GEORGE BEST:
A MEMOIR

GEORGE BEST:
A MEMOIR

MICHAEL PARKINSON

and Michael Parkinson Jnr

HODDER &
STOUGHTON

First published in Great Britain in 2018 by Hodder & Stoughton
An Hachette UK company

3

Copyright © Michael Parkinson 2018

A CIP catalogue record for this title is available from the British Library

Hardback ISBN 9781473675735
Trade Paperback ISBN 9781473675759
eBook ISBN 9781473675742

Typeset in Garamond by Palimpsest Book Production Ltd, Falkirk, Stirlingshire

Printed and bound in Great Britain by Clays Ltd, Elcograf S.p.A.

Hodder & Stoughton policy is to use papers that are natural, renewable
and recyclable products and made from wood grown in sustainable forests.
The logging and manufacturing processes are expected to conform to the
environmental regulations of the country of origin.

Hodder & Stoughton Ltd
Carmelite House
50 Victoria Embankment
London EC4Y 0DZ

www.hodder.co.uk

My son Mike has worked with me as a producer of radio and TV shows for the past fifteen years and lately has been interviewing me on our touring stage shows. He also provided invaluable research and insights into the book I wrote about Muhammad Ali. With this book, because he almost came to regard George as a member of the family he provided a lot more than ideas and encouragement. He has his own chapter on George at the end of the book but, truth be told, his insights into a complex personality provided me with a clear picture of an often complex relationship. I am proud to say that this is his book as much as mine.

CONTENTS

George Best — 'born with something a little bit special'.

PROLOGUE

'George Best was sometimes a difficult man to defend in the aftermath of a drunken episode. What was never a problem was to talk of his genius as a player and to love him as a friend. That was easy.'

From my obituary of George Best
in the *Daily Telegraph*, 2005

THIS book is a testament to the significant role George Best played in my life. I was one of the first to write about him when I saw him make his debut for Manchester United against West Bromwich Albion in 1963. As a journalist, you're always looking for inspiration, for somebody or something that lifts the sport you're covering out of the ordinary, and when I watched him in that game I knew I had found it.

I first met him when he was seventeen and sucking a sweet. It was 1963 in Manchester and the city tingled with expectation that this footballer with the physique of a toothpick might be something special. I asked him what he thought about his sudden fame, about the sacks of unopened mail cluttering the bedroom in his digs. He gave me a sly look from under long, black lashes. 'Very nice,' he said and popped another sweet into his mouth.

In the next forty years or more, to the time he died, we were friends. I interviewed him more than a dozen times, wrote a book about him, watched his glorious triumphs, visited him in prison. He sometimes stayed at our house seeking refuge from the pursuing media. He always arrived with a football for the kids and played with them on the lawn.

I interviewed him on his fiftieth birthday and, looking back, he tried to answer the question posed in the most famous George Best anecdote of them all: 'Where did it all go wrong?' He said, 'All of a sudden, as a teenager from Belfast, I had to employ three full-time secretaries to answer 10,000 letters a week. I didn't know how to cope, nor did anyone else. In those days footballers didn't have people to protect and advise them.'

The ultimate irony of George Best's career was that although his gifts and looks made him the perfect product for his time, and he was exploited as such, no one thought how to protect him. Not long before George died, I brought him together with David Beckham on *Parkinson*. Beckham, the Rolls-Royce product of a system designed to seduce the worlds of soccer and showbiz. Best, by comparison, careworn and scuffed by his passage through life, the pioneer who made the trip more or less on his own and in little more than a covered wagon. While acknowledging the problems he encountered on his way, George never blamed anyone but himself. One of his most attractive traits was a complete lack of self-pity. He hated it when people discussed his life as a tragedy, insisting the good times outnumbered the bad.

What I soon realised, and I wasn't the only one, was that George didn't want saving. Matt Busby, who loved him but could never work him out, once said to me, 'I keep having this terrible thought that one day George will end it all. That he'll commit suicide.' He was right. It just took him longer than either of us thought. I once asked George if he would change anything about his life.

'Nothing. I've had a great time,' he said. It's easy to scoff at such an obvious fib from a man who sometimes gave every indication he would have been an excellent kamikaze pilot. Yet I often observed that the friends who took him out for a meal to appeal to his common sense and offer him advice about a more sensible lifestyle usually returned much worse for wear than George.

We who thought we could change his ways, who could help him stop drinking, came to understand that in the final analysis he didn't want to stop. He told me that a counsellor once said to him, 'You are at the stage when you have to choose. Do you switch the light on or off?' And George chose the latter. Why? The easy explanation was that he was a chronic alcoholic. That's what killed him, but *why* did he drink so much?

In all the time I knew him, and all the hours we talked, he never said. He would sidestep the question with a joke. But drinking didn't make him happy. So why? I used to think it was because he was bored that his talent and looks made everything and everyone fall at his feet. He was a supremely gifted athlete who found playing football a simple matter. So was finding a mate. Women offered themselves and he took them. Simple as that. No sweat. He was a highly intelligent man but had little truck with introspection. But I also suspect that there was within him a profound melancholy not altogether attributable to Celtic gloom.

A few weeks before his death, he came to the Royal Oak, my son Nick's restaurant, for a reunion with his Manchester United team-mates. He didn't drink at all that evening and next day called to say he'd had a marvellous time. I told him that was because he was sober for a change. He laughed, and it was the last time we spoke.

George Best died in the early hours of 25 November 2005 at the Cromwell Hospital in London. He was fifty-nine. The news saddened millions and surprised no one. I missed my friend's funeral. I was abroad at the time. But I watched the television coverage and felt ashamed at not being there and even more remorseful that I had not visited him in hospital. I had been persuaded not to visit by friends who had been deeply saddened and shocked by the experience.

However, for the most part, whenever I think about George I find myself smiling.

When people ask me what he was like I suggest they look at the portrait reproduced in this book which places George against the agitated background of the crowd that worshipped him and yet shows him to be an almost shadowy and nostalgic figure.

That was George, forever at the centre of things, living in the spotlight yet curiously alone and, I think, lonely.

When he died, I wrote, 'In the forty years since he made his debut as a footballer George Best played for glory in the European Cup final and for a few quid in a scruffy paddock to buy a drink or two. He knew what it was like to live like a millionaire and slop out in prison. He went to bed with a thousand beautiful girls and ended up so lonely he tried to kill himself. He was hailed as the first pop superstar of football and became a terminal drunk. Whatever we make of his life, it wasn't predictable, and while defending him was sometimes difficult, loving him never was.'

But when your children ask how great a player he was, simply tell them there was no one quite like him, not before and most certainly not since. Sir Matt Busby, who knew a thing or two about footballers, said that what made George unique was that he excelled in every outfield position. He could defend or attack with great skill, pass or shoot with precision, was equally adept with either foot, and possessed speed, intelligence and an unquenchable competitive spirit. Moreover, he was fearless and had the balance of a steeplejack. He loved the big arena. He was a great star. There remains one unanswered question. He gave up the game aged twenty-seven, before he reached his prime, and despite various attempts to rekindle his career, both here and in the States, it was never the same – his lifestyle ensured it never could be. The question always remains – how great could he have been? The ultimate sadness is that not even George Best knew the answer to that.

And yet, despite him being a fascinating enigma, despite never discovering the reason for his helter-skelter journey of self-destruction, despite all the shared experience and the affection I have for him, this was a surprisingly difficult book to write.

One of the main reasons was that his life had already been picked over and scrutinised in painstaking detail and with varying quality in books, documentaries and even feature films. Indeed, I had already pitched my cap into that particular ring when, in 1975, I wrote one of the first biographies of George, called *Best: An Intimate Biography*. Most recently and notably, that meticulous biographer of sporting greats Duncan Hamilton has written a detailed and forensic examination of his life. So my initial thought, when faced with the task, was what more could I add?

On top of that, I had always felt uncomfortable about revisiting his life story. To think of writing another book whilst he was alive and intent upon a very public suicide was too much for me. I would've felt disloyal, voyeuristic, and anyway, watching him destroy himself from afar was so painful that we gradually drifted apart. It was an unconscious mutual decision; no words were needed. Our lives and lifestyles had become so different. In any case, he never liked me to see him at his worst, and I found it too upsetting to witness his descent into a personal hell and the inevitable conclusion of his lifestyle. After many attempts, I finally had to accept that I could no longer help him; he had chosen his path. He wanted to be left alone and I respected that decision. Even after his death it didn't feel right. There was the feeling that perhaps as his friend, who got as close to him as anyone could, I should just let him rest in peace and not become part of the media knitting brigade at the scaffold.

But – and with journalists there is always a but – in the intervening years since writing the biography I'd been nagged by a desire to update and reassess the thoughts and conclusions I had come to in that book. There is much in it that still resonates with me today, but knowing what I know now and witnessing some of it, I wanted to finish off the picture I began painting when we all still believed that George would be back in football, maybe even in a Manchester United shirt, once he grew bored of a life without that which defined him and the dust of his chaotic private life calmed down. Upon reading it again, what also struck me, and in a way is more remarkable, was that it was published at all. In those days biographies about footballers were rare beasts. It was a testament to the public's fascination with all things George and the foresight of my long-term publisher, Roddy Bloomfield, who has always championed the genre of sporting biography in the UK, that it saw the light of day.

That book was the result of a year spent in George's company chronicling his life since he had arrived as a skinny, cripplingly shy fifteen-year-old from a housing estate in Belfast, blessed with a talent that not even he could fully explain. It is a combination of my observations and transcripts of conversations I had with George at the time. The format allows the reader to observe the different viewpoints expressed about the same events by two men who were close friends but also very different people, at different stages of their lives. I was forty, married with three kids, forging ahead with my career in television. George was twenty-nine, an unrepentant playboy but at a crossroads in both his life and career. In the book, George recounted every up and down of his extraordinary journey with the same lack of introspection or self-criticism that he exhibited for most of his life, while I played the role of the older, slightly indulgent, brother, not afraid to offer opinions and express criticism, but always in the spirit of concern and affection.

At the end of the book my overall feeling and conclusion was that George seemed for the most part content to leave football behind and concentrate on being a businessman and the owner, with his best friend and confidant, Malcolm Wagner, of the infamous Slack Alice nightclub in Manchester, rather than the most famous and possibly the greatest footballer on the planet. There was also a belief that what was causing the problem was his disenchantment with football, and in particular the way Manchester United had declined since 1968, plus the goldfish bowl his life had become. There was no real sense from George of any regret at what had transpired, nor much worry about how his life was panning out. It was only the author, along with Best's legion of other fans, who felt a sense of justifiable disappointment that we would possibly never again see this graceful, brave and gilded athlete in his proper habitat. And although the book is not full of prescience – who could have foreseen the chaos that was to come? – there was also concern that his lifestyle was becoming unhealthy and self-destructive. There was, however, a genuine hope that, freed from the demands of a game he had fallen out of love with, he would find a roadmap for his life that didn't involve driving at high speed down dead ends. Some hope.

It is a particularly apposite time to be writing about George: 2018 marks two significant anniversaries in his story. It is the fiftieth anniversary of Manchester United winning the European Cup, back when it was a proper cup competition and not a UEFA-backed fifth-column attempt to introduce a European Super League under our noses. It is also the fiftieth anniversary of George being crowned as the European Player of the Year, an award given at a time when football was a proper game, played by . . . I'll stop now: that's for another book, another time. In 1968 George was at the peak of his powers, the zenith of his fame. He was a superstar; girls loved him and men admired him. Yet from that point on, his life began to unravel.

It is also the sixtieth anniversary of the Munich air disaster, the terrible, avoidable tragedy that decimated Sir

*George savours the moment as Manchester United celebrate the 1968
European Cup victory that finally realised Sir Matt Busby's dream.*

George in full flight – the greatest player I have ever seen.

Matt Busby's first great team and sent him on a messianic mission of redemption, driven by a crushing guilt, to build another team and avenge the deaths of his 'Babes'. A devout Catholic, Sir Matt had built his first church on the rock of Duncan Edwards. Now that Duncan was lost to him, Sir Matt was looking for another rock. Enter George Best.

As in my recent book about Muhammad Ali, I'm going to combine my thoughts about George's life with excerpts from the television interviews I did with him (sadly only four out of five survive, but more of that later) as well as interviews with other people, like Sir Matt and Sir Bobby Charlton. I'm also going to revisit the first book I wrote on George, which has much in it that is still relevant. The current book differs from the Ali book in that it is not a detailed biography, but more a look at the forces, both within and without, that shaped and defined George and ultimately led him down such a destructive road. But it is also a book about a time and a place which I was lucky enough to experience and which, without him realising it was created and personified by George Best.

It is a story with a mythic tone. A young boy touched by the gods, led to a destiny he had little control over.

Chapter 1

MY FOOTBALLING LIFE

'Some people believe football is a matter of life and death.
I'm very disappointed with that attitude. I can assure you it
is much, much more important than that.'

Bill Shankly

LOOKING back after more than eighty years, it is difficult to get a true picture of what went on. Life seen through the distorting picture of fading memory. Yet certain things remain clear enough. With me, it is retracing the steps which led me to the moment I became enraptured by a game. I can still remember diving full-length through deep grass and a cowpat to take a catch when I was eleven and making my debut in league cricket, playing with men. The onrushing team-mates who sought an embrace backed off when they saw me covered in manure. I can recall scoring my first goal for Darfield Road Juniors, the ball bouncing off my shin pad and into the net, a clumsy, fortuitous goal which the local paper nonetheless described as 'a well-placed left-foot shot from schoolboy Michael

Parkinson making a promising debut in the senior league'. I remember the phrase because I wrote it.

Most of all, I can remember the first time my father took me to see Barnsley play. I recall the slog from the bus station to the brow of the hill, the first sight of Oakwell and the beginning of a lifelong addiction to soccer. That was in 1940. My father told me later that at half-time he asked me what I thought, and I said it was all right, but I wanted to go home. He insisted I stay, committing me to a lifetime of watching, playing and writing about the game. Looking back, I have been aware of how fortunate I was to have lived through an era when the game changed from the days of my dad digging coal alongside colleagues who played for Barnsley on a Saturday, to a time when a combination of wealth and celebrity gave players riches and fame beyond imagining. It has been like watching a two-up, two-down in central London being replaced by the Shard.

Over the years I have enjoyed writing about my beloved Barnsley and the joy and humour of it all without understanding that the reason why I became addicted to the joy and humour of it all was because of the joy and humour of it all. The body warmth of the crowd on the terrace, the smell of Woodbines and last night's beer. The memories, many of them apocryphal, that have passed into folklore. Like the time one of our defenders, suspected of heavy drinking, walked backwards to take a free kick and fell into the terrace. As the ref ran over to assess the damage, a fan shouted, 'Leave him be, ref, he needs a rest.' The time the trainer, running onto the field to treat an injured player the crowd believed was faking injury, was advised, 'Don't revive him, bury the sod.' Most remarkable of all, the comment of the Chesterfield fan standing next to our group when Tommy Capel – the Chesterfield skipper – decided to nominate his brother to take a penalty which would decide the match. The brother missed by a mile and, as the ball sailed into the Spion Kop, the Chesterfield supporter was heard to exclaim, 'Nepotism, bloody nepotism.' Generally speaking, the section of the terraces we frequented in those days was, at best, a two-syllable neighbourhood. It took until the next home game for assiduous research to reveal what was meant, after which we used the word more and more, sometimes without quite making sense. For instance, when our centre forward George Robledo was signed by Newcastle, Uncle Jim, who liked playing with words, defined the player's insistence that Newcastle also sign brother Ted as 'nepo-tistic'. We nodded our heads in sympathetic agreement as our neighbours regarded us with a mixture of bafflement and awe.

Over the years of falling in love with Barnsley I am aware I might have concentrated too much on the hard men who guarded the citadel rather than the artists who adorned it. Even though in far Kuala Lumpur a Skinner Normanton Appreciation Society was formed in honour of the man who relished the task of protecting his team-mates with a dedicated fervour such as would see their opponents ending up in the third row of the stand, nothing Skinner achieved pleased me as much as the succession of creative playmakers, often short of stature and with slightly bandy legs, who delighted with sleight of foot and nimble brain to feed tricky wingers and goal-scoring centre forwards. Players like Jimmy Baxter and Steve Griffiths, wingers like Johnny Kelly and Arthur Kaye, centre forwards like Cec McCormack and George Robledo and Tommy Taylor. But for me the greatest hero of my young life was Danny Blanchflower.

Barnsley bought him from Glentoran for £6,000, a fee sufficient to make Danny concerned he might not be up to the job in a club then doing OK in the Second Division of the English League. He loved recounting the story of his first practice match facing a tough-looking team-mate with the ball at his feet running towards him. As Blanchflower pondered on which side his opponent would try to pass him, he just kept coming, flattened Danny and left him to count the stud marks on his chest. That was Blanchflower's introduction to Skinner and to Barnsley, a team he transformed.

We had seen nothing like the way he passed the ball, dominated the flow and style of play, revealing the intelligence he later brought to his time with Ireland, his great Spurs team and, after finishing playing, his perceptive observations on the game in the media. He was a truly fascinating and inspiring man who I both admired as a player and philosopher about the game and loved as a friend. He never tired of telling the story of how he was taken in the Barnsley chairman's car to a hotel in Birmingham and made to eat in the kitchen while in the dining room Barnsley agreed to sell him to Aston Villa for £14,500. In his later life, Danny became the forlorn victim of a cruel illness.

When he left Barnsley, a lanky young centre forward was climbing the beanstalk in Barnsley's youth and reserve teams. He was Tommy Taylor and the talk was of a true star in the making. The rumour was that Matt Busby, then team-rebuilding at Manchester United, was an admirer. The youngster was in the Alhambra Cinema in Barnsley when an emergency message was flashed on the screen asking Mr Tommy Taylor to report to Oakwell immediately to talk to his manager. That led to him joining the Busby Babes, enhancing his reputation as one of England's very best centre forwards and gaining international honours – before perishing in the Munich air disaster.

And then there I was, outside Old Trafford at the first game after Munich in 1958, trying to make sense of it all, thinking about the path that had brought me to that place and wondering what the future held. What or who was the next link in a fascinating chain of events which had taken me from Oakwell to Old Trafford, from a crush on the terraces to the press box, to pontificating on TV and meeting my heroes? If it had stopped there, it would have seemed sufficient. But as I entertained thoughts of how lucky I had been, I had no idea that in Belfast a young lad was already demonstrating an exceptional talent. His name was George Best and after he arrived in Manchester nothing was the same again.

But George's story begins way before he first stepped out onto the Old Trafford pitch. The course of his life and career was set and framed by one tragedy, one man and one town – Munich, Matt and Manchester – without which the story might have been very different. So let's start at the very beginning. It's five years before George makes his debut for Manchester United. We're inside an aircraft on a slush-covered runway at Munich-Riem airport, with Sir Matt and his Babes, plus assorted journalists and club dignitaries. The atmosphere is tense, the passengers nervous, as the aircraft begins its third attempt to take off.

Chapter 2

MUNICH

United's flag is deepest red
It shrouded all our Munich dead
Before their limbs grew stiff and cold
Their heart's blood dyed its ev'ry fold
Then raise United's banner high
Beneath its shade we'll live and die
So keep the faith and never fear
We'll keep the Red Flag flying here
We'll never die, we'll never die
We'll never die, we'll never die
We'll keep the Red flag flying high
'Cos Man United will never die.

Stretford End song

Hɪsᴛᴏʀʏ is full of what-ifs. What if Munich had never happened? The team that was destroyed by that crash were, in Sir Matt Busby's opinion, the best he ever assembled. I know this because he told me so when I interviewed him in 1973:

Edited excerpt from interview with Sir Matt Busby (Parkinson, 1973)

MICHAEL: A lot of people would say that was the best club side there's ever been. Would you go along with that?

MATT: Well, I had the feeling they were going to be the best club side. They were the best club side I've seen in Britain. They were young. They'd won the championship. A couple of championships. They were just maturing. The future of English football, I think, was in their hands. I think the next few years they probably would've won everything it was possible to win. It was a great, great side. The best league side, the best club side, I've seen.

So, what if Matt's prediction had come true and they had gone on to mature into the best club side he had ever seen? What if the great Duncan Edwards, still in his early twenties, years from his peak as a footballer but even at twenty-one, in terms of skill and physicality, the dominant

Duncan Edwards – the Rock Busby built his babes on.

player of his generation, destined to be a superstar, had survived? What would have been the story of George Best then? Would Busby, without the need for the immediate reconstruction of his team, still have made Best the fulcrum of his side, placing huge demands and expectations upon such slim shoulders and such a fragile personality? Or would he have taken things more slowly, more carefully – bringing George through under the radar whilst his Babes, led by Edwards, now recognised as the best player in the world, swept all before them? A protected George Best allowed to grow and mature away from the limelight – what might have been the story of George then?

But Munich happened. Twenty-three people lost their lives, including eight of the Busby Babes, whilst an eleven-year-old Best with a ball at his feet ran rings round his friends under the lamplight of the Cregagh Estate, dreaming of being the best player in the world. He was not to know that this tragedy would change his life for ever.

The events of that fateful day are almost too painful to recount. Manchester United are returning from qualifying for the semi-finals of the European Cup after drawing 3–3 with Red Star Belgrade to win 5–4 on aggregate. The plane has stopped at Munich to refuel. It is a cold, snowy day. Slush on the runway, the winter day fading to a close in the early afternoon. There have already been two failed take-off attempts, the captain complaining of a problem with one of his engines. Resigned, the passengers return to the departure lounge. A relieved Duncan Edwards sends a telegram to his landlady: 'All flights cancelled. Flying home tomorrow. Duncan.' Then, unexpectedly, they are asked to reboard. At 3.04 p.m. on Thursday, 6 February 1958, another attempt to take off is made. The plane never gets enough height and crashes into a fence and then a house, exploding into flames.

Alongside Busby's Babes, fifteen other poor souls were lost, with Busby himself left critically ill in hospital. One of the survivors was Bobby Charlton. He escaped the crash with only minor cuts after being thrown clear of the wreckage. But the mental scars of that day ran so deep in him that it wasn't until I interviewed him in 2007 that he felt he could at last talk about it. He had written his autobiography and for the first time he addressed the feelings about Munich that he had bottled up for so long. What he revealed was a man racked by the guilt of having survived when so many of his team-mates were lost.

*Edited excerpt from interview with Sir Bobby Charlton (*Parkinson, *2007)*

MICHAEL: You say in the book that Munich defined you.

BOBBY: Yes.

MICHAEL: That you would have to, if you wrote the book, face those ghosts.

BOBBY: Yes.

MICHAEL: And how difficult was that?

BOBBY: Well, it's not so bad now. It's not so bad now. But there were lots of times when people were saying, why don't you write? You've got this fantastic story of what happened to you at Munich, and what happened to you afterwards. And I felt that it just wasn't the time. It was really personal. I didn't want to talk about Munich and offend some of the relatives. And then eventually it got to the stage where almost everybody was asking me to do it. And I thought, 'Well, I'd better just get this off my chest.' And I did, and I felt really better after I'd done it.

MICHAEL: But you also say in the book that you carried with you for a while a sense of guilt.

BOBBY: Well, I felt, why me? Why am I here with nothing? Nothing happened to me other than a little gash on the head. And all these other friends had been killed. I felt this is not fair, why should it be me? It took a long time for me to feel better about it. And it was such a momentous event, you know. For so many young people to die, just on the verge of the great success that was ahead of them. And I just couldn't understand why. I realise it was partly because of the design of the aircraft. Half the seats were facing forward, and half the seats were facing backwards. And all the ones that had their back to the front of the aeroplane were the ones that survived.

MICHAEL: Oh really? So you had your back to the impact?

BOBBY: Harry Gregg . . . they didn't lose any consciousness at all. They had to go back into the aeroplane, and do things I couldn't possibly have done myself, I don't think.

MICHAEL: And you walked away from it, didn't you?

BOBBY: Well, we walked away and we couldn't, I couldn't believe it. I couldn't believe it. I was maybe in a little bit of concussion. But a few days later, when you realise exactly what happened and the enormity of what happened, then you start thinking about how lucky you've been. And I was so lucky.

MICHAEL: Did you have to have any kind of counselling or anything like that?

BOBBY: No. No, no, no.

MICHAEL: You saw yourself through it, did you?

BOBBY: Yes. I went to the first match after Munich. I was in hospital for just short of two weeks, I think. And when I came back, they were preparing for the next round of the FA Cup, against Sheffield Wednesday.

MICHAEL: I was there.

BOBBY: My uncle Tommy had a car, and my dad and myself, we came down to see the match. Because they had told me, 'Just stay away as long as you wish, Bobby. Come back when you're ready.' And when I got to the match, and I saw the effort they were putting in, all the young players, Harry Gregg and Bill Foulkes, I thought, 'What am I doing? There's nothing wrong with me.' So I said to Jimmy Murphy, 'I've got to go back to see the doctor tomorrow, but I'll be back on Friday.' And I came back, and the enormity of it . . .

It was left for people to actually make sure that their name remained, you know. The players who died, their names remain. And the only way you could satisfy everyone really was to win the European Cup again for them. Because they'd been trying their best to win it. And we would have won it with them. And, well, it was just momentous, you know, for so many young players.

Bobby's reaction is the classic response of a survivor of such an event, a sense that he had done something wrong by surviving whilst his close friends and team-mates did not. Though he questioned his courage on the night, it actually takes real courage to pick yourself up from such an event and realise that there are bigger issues at stake than your personal feelings.

*

Munich was full of stories of lucky escapes. One of the most extraordinary I came across was when I was researching for a one-man show with the late, great broadcaster John Arlott. In 1958 he was working as a football correspondent for the *Guardian* when he was unexpectedly offered the chance to go and see Manchester United play Red Star Belgrade:

Edited excerpt from interview with John Arlott (Parkinson, 1981)

MICHAEL: Going back just for a moment to the period when you were on the *Guardian* and you were covering soccer. You worked alongside H. D. Davies, Donny Davies, who was killed in the Munich air crash. And I didn't know until I started doing the research on you for this, that you were due to be on that same aeroplane.

JOHN: Yes, you see I was writing the Friday leads on soccer for the *Guardian*. Nobody had ever lasted on that job for more than a season before. You had to write a thousand-word feature for a Friday about football that had happened the previous Saturday, and that was a difficult thing to do consistently. One day I rang Larry Montague, the sports editor in Manchester. In those days, it was very much the *Manchester Guardian*: Manchester-orientated.

And I said, 'Larry, you know, if I'm going to write this feature, I must see some continental football. It's important, it's happening. Manchester United are there and all England is thinking about this, and I must get a look at it.' So he said, 'If Donny wants to go, Donny will go. Donny is the correspondent, you're the number two. He has the first pick.' So I said, 'OK, OK, OK, I can only tell you that I can't write these leaders properly until I've seen football being played on the continent.'

Eventually he rang me up and he said, 'Look, Donny can't go to the game next week. Will you go and see Manchester United play Arsenal on Saturday? Write it for me for Monday, in terms of what they've got to face on the following Wednesday, and then I've got the tickets for you. Everything's ready, you can go over and see it.' So I said, 'Well, thank you very much indeed.' 'Don't thank me,' he said. 'It's all right.' So I rang up on Sunday to check my copy, and they said, 'Mr Montague wants to speak to you.' I said, 'Hello, Larry, what is it?' He said, 'I'm sorry, Donny has found out that he can go after all – to Budapest – and he's going.' I said, well, I said . . . I can't really repeat in front of your sensitive public what I said. He said, 'Donny's the correspondent. If he wants to go, he goes.' I said, 'All right.'

So this really got me down, and on the following Thursday, I said to my secretary, later my wife, I said,

'Look, this has got me down, I'm going out.' She said, 'Where are you going?' I said, 'I'm going to buy a book.' So I pushed off and went to one bookshop after another. I ended up in Rota's in Vigo Street. Miss Jones came out and said, 'There's a phone call for you, Mr Arlott.' I said, 'Impossible, nobody knows I'm here.' She said, 'Well, it's a phone call for you.' So I went out and took the call. It was Valerie and she said, 'Larry Montague's been on the phone. He wants you to get down to the Fleet Street offices as fast as you can. The Manchester United plane has crashed. Be prepared to write the obits as the chits come in, and start with Donny Davies.' I said, 'Oh, my God.' I mean, I should have been sitting in his seat if he hadn't decided at the last minute he could go.

Subsequently, Larry Montague wanted to do a book of Donny's contributions on football for the *Guardian* and asked if I would write a foreword for it. I said, 'Yes, I would be very proud to.' And then it transpired that Mrs Davies said she would not allow me to touch or have anything to do with a book of her husband's. I've always wondered if he had told her, in order to go, that I'd refused to go, or something like that, and that it was my fault. Because nobody could blame me for him being on the plane, I wanted to be on it myself. Not afterwards.

MICHAEL: Extraordinary thing. What were your feelings when you thought about it later? Was it just good luck or what?

JOHN: It was barmy luck. I heaved a great sigh and thought, 'Thank God.' And then the next chance I had to get on an aeroplane, I jumped on it.

All this was happening whilst Matt Busby lay in hospital close to death. Such was his condition that he had no knowledge of what had happened. When I interviewed him in 1973, I asked him when he first became aware of what had taken place.

Edited excerpt from interview with Sir Matt Busby
(Parkinson, 1973)

MICHAEL: This horrifying thing that happened at the crash in Munich, which destroyed this team that you'd built up. Was there a moment in hospital when you were told what had happened? Was there a moment when you felt like giving it all up? Felt like dying – you wanted to die?

MATT: Yes. I was periodically coming round and going back. And after the best part of three weeks, I suddenly realised a terrible thing had happened. And, of course, the chief of the hospital had forbidden everybody to go in and talk to me about it. But a nurse walked in one day and said, 'Duncan Edwards has died.' So when I heard this, I couldn't rest. I said to my wife, 'You've got to tell me.' And when

I said a name, she either nodded, meaning he'd gone, or shook her head.

So with this, I lost all real feeling for life, and I felt as though I wanted to die, because I was so obsessed. I felt that probably, in a way, I may have been responsible for this. That I shouldn't have allowed us to go the third time. But you can't tell the experts that. If anyone came to tell me about football management, then I would say he was a fool. So I was a fool if I went and told the pilot what to do. But I did feel that way for a time.

MICHAEL: I must tell you, I travelled with you, the first time you flew that airline again after the crash, which was to Madrid, in the semi-final of the European Cup, and you could feel the tension on the plane. You must have been very aware of it at the time. I sat next to Bobby Charlton, who was like this . . . [EYES CLOSED] But what made the whole thing marvellous and memorable for me was that when we landed at Madrid airport, the players all started clapping. It was an extraordinary relief of tension.

Sir Matt was never the same man after the accident. He was profoundly affected by Munich, both physically and mentally. Physically, he had been terribly injured. He was twice given the last rites. His chest was crushed, his lung was punctured, his ankle badly broken, and he had awful wounds along his back and ribs. For the rest of his life he would be plagued by pain and fragile health.

On top of this, he was almost destroyed mentally. No amount of reasoning could alter the fact that he felt guilty and responsible for the deaths of the members of the team he had created, and in particular the loss of a once-in-a-lifetime player, Duncan Edwards. It had been his idea, against the wishes of the Football Association, to enter the European Cup. It may have been for the right reasons, given that ever since Puskás orchestrated the Mighty Magyars' 7–1 demolition of England in 1954 Busby knew that the future of how football would and should be played lay abroad, but it didn't stop him feeling a crushing and debilitating sense of responsibility. He felt his bloody-mindedness had put his players in unnecessary danger. No wonder, as he lay stricken in his hospital bed, enveloped by an oxygen tent, that he prayed for death.

Yet for whatever reason, and his deep and sincere faith should not be underestimated as a factor, it was at this nadir of his life that from somewhere he dredged up the courage to turn aside such thoughts and vowed to honour his lost team. Driven by a strong sense of shame that he had nearly given up, even though he had been spared while others lost their lives, he knew that if any good was to come out of this tragedy, he would have to personally ensure that the young, bright and gifted players that had lost their lives would not be remembered by inanimate, cold memorials of stone or bronze, but by something more tangible and meaningful. That team, his first great team, were on the cusp of something special – of winning the European Cup and dominating English football. Because of Munich, there was unfinished business, and what better way to avenge that shocking and senseless loss than to rebuild a team in their image and win the trophy their talent deserved?

But, romantic as he was about the purpose and meaning of football to the average fan, Busby was also a pragmatist. This was not going to be an easy task. His Babes were built around one supreme talent. The other players were much more than simple hewers of wood and carriers of water, yet they were still just talented members of a court that served King Duncan. Bobby Charlton, gifted and irreplaceable as he was, wasn't the answer. He was the conductor, not a maestro. Another collection of talented courtiers he could find. But Duncan had been the key – and now Matt had lost it.

So Busby lay in his bed and plotted, haunted by ghosts, as a young George Best lay in his bed with a football by his side and dreamt of sporting immortality, whilst taking every waking moment to hone the skills that Busby could only dream of and hope for. Two people unaware of each other yet hurtling towards a common destiny. The stage was set.

Chapter 3

THE HOUSE THAT MATT BUILT

If ever they're playing in your town,
You must get to that football ground.
Take a lesson, come to see,
Football taught by Matt Busby.

Manchester,
Manchester United.
A bunch of bouncing 'Busby Babes',
They deserve to be knighted.

From a calypso by Edric Connor,
recorded in 1955

I N 2017 Manchester United replaced Real Madrid as the richest club in the world. They had a revenue of over £600 million and an estimated worth of around $2.2 billion. They are now a global brand with legions of fans in every corner of the planet. There hardly seems to be a TV report from anywhere in the world, even when talking about some natural disaster, without one person, be they man or woman, ninety or nine, incongruously sporting a Manchester United shirt emblazoned with the name of the latest superstar signing.

On the pitch and over the years, they have become a byword for attractive and free-flowing football, and though in recent times they have mutated into more of a multi-national conglomerate than a football club, there is still an air of glamour about Manchester United, its stadium commonly known as the Theatre of Dreams. But it was not always so. The success and footballing culture that underlies the monolith that is Manchester United was started by one man: Sir Matt Busby.

Busby became synonymous with Manchester United. During his many years as manager, director and president, until his death in 1994, he built outstanding success from bare bones. When he arrived as manager in 1945 the stadium was a heap of rubble. There was no training

'What you see now is what Sir Matt Busby designed' – Old Trafford in 1945 and, opposite, the modern stadium.

ground and his first office was a Nissen hut costing £30. Yet, twenty-three years later he had made it one of the richest and most admired clubs in the land, had personally won unequalled success and reputation on the field of play and, perhaps more significantly, had hung on to his job while 600 of his fellow managers were being sacked. By 1969 he was the last remaining manager of a First Division club undisturbed since 1945.

His success was built upon a desire to innovate, to assimilate ideas and approaches that were working in other

countries and in other sports apart from football. When I interviewed Sir Bobby, I asked him about Matt's influence.

Edited excerpt from interview with Sir Bobby Charlton (Parkinson, 2007)

BOBBY: Well, he was a marvellous man. Old Trafford is now the most fantastic stadium. Beautiful stadium. And Sir Matt Busby started this a long, long time ago. He got lots of young players, under sixteen years of age, and put them in the first team, which was unheard of. And he went to the United States – and when he came back, he said, 'We are going to change Manchester United, the ground. I've seen things that are happening in the United States which will eventually come to Europe, and we have to be first.' And we built the new stand. What you see now is what Sir Matt Busby designed.

MICHAEL: And the philosophy of football too. It was an attacking, pleasing game of football.

BOBBY: Absolutely. When I eventually got into the first team and he gave his team talk, he said, 'We're in Trafford Park, the largest industrial estate in Europe. And the people that work there, when they finish work at the end of the week, they want to go and see something a little bit different and a little exciting.' He said, 'So you have the responsibility.

The people that work on the shop floor, they've worked really hard, so you have to give them their little bit of entertainment.'

Manchester United playing in Europe was such an adventure. We were going to play places we'd never heard of. We didn't know the players. There was only one club, Real Madrid, who had Di Stéfano and Gento, that you really knew. All the others were strange. And Matt Busby said we had to do it. Even against the wishes of the Football League, he went into Europe. He said, 'It's the future. This is what the public want to see.'

Sir Bobby's assessment reveals the combination of visionary and romantic that was Sir Matt. He saw that football was becoming a truly world game and that the way to keep constantly improving was to play abroad. Yet, at the same time, he never forgot the importance of a football club to the fans and the local area. He understood that if football had any purpose it was to entertain, to take away the cares and worries of the average working man for ninety minutes by sending out teams of players equipped with the skills to express themselves in an imaginative style, unfettered by the restraints of tactical systems. He felt it was beholden upon him to teach and play 'the beautiful game', particularly at a time when the style of football was becoming somewhat prosaic.

As early as 1960 he was quoted as saying, 'Without wishing to belittle the achievements of any club, I believe certain methods of attaining success have influenced British football too much, and in the wrong direction. I am thinking of the power game. Results are achieved by placing too much emphasis on speed, power and physical fitness. Such teams now have many imitators. We are breeding a number of teams whose outlook seems to be that pace, punch and fitness are all that is required to win all the honours in the game. They forget that without pure skills, these virtues count for precisely nothing. I should like to see the honours in England won by a pure footballing side, the sort of team that concentrates on ball skills above all else.'

Busby's philosophy was simple, it was built on youth: 'If they are good enough, they are old enough.' He admired managers who built teams that expressed themselves. He believed in creating a team of players who could attack and defend as one. It was Total Football before that phrase was coined. There were no pre-match talks full of opposition-player dossiers or patterns of play indicated by magnetic discs on a whiteboard; no sticking rigidly to 4–2–4 or, since Ramsey's success, the in-favour 4–3–3 'Wingless Wonders'. The players were told to go out and express themselves, the work of moulding them into a collective whole done on the training ground under the steely gaze of Busby's coach and right-hand man, Jimmy Murphy, about whom the great Sir Bobby said, 'Whatever I achieved in football, I owe to one man and only one man.' Murphy was crucial to Busby's vision. While Busby stood on the bridge directing the ship, Murphy drilled the crew. He also managed to keep the

The team behind the team: Sir Matt Busby and Jimmy Murphy.

boiler well stoked. During his time at the club Murphy brought through to the first team over seventy players he scouted for and developed in the Manchester United youth system. They may have been Busby's Babes, but they definitely had two parents.

But, and as I write in the 1975 book about George, Busby's achievements were not altogether to be measured in terms of longevity and cups. He had brought a new style to football management.

In the forties and fifties managers of soccer clubs were prey to the foibles of their boards of directors who were, in the main, well-meaning men, but ignorant of soccer. Often they interfered in matters of team selection, thereby making the manager's job impossible.

Len Shackleton, a great soccer player with an irrepressible sense of humour, summed up this period in his autobiography when under a heading, 'The average director's knowledge of soccer', he left a blank page.

Busby demanded, and received, a free hand from his directors. The running of the team was his concern and his alone. Louis Edwards, United's chairman and a firm friend and fan of Matt, says: 'He had a marvellous arrangement with us. I'd tell the board, "Matt's made up his mind but he's coming to us for advice."'

What this all meant was that by the time Matt began rebuilding from the wreckage of Munich, he had a club that in structure and philosophy was cast in his own image – the ideal home for a fifteen-year-old Best crossing the Irish Sea, battling both sea- and homesickness, to display and hone his talents. Without knowing who his most famous actor would be, Busby had prepared the perfect stage and footballing culture for the man who would become the King of Manchester, with his court at Old Trafford. If Busby built Manchester United, Best created the brand. He, more than any other United player, truly made Old Trafford the Theatre of Dreams.

Chapter 4

BEST THE PLAYER

'With feet as sensitive as a pickpocket's hands, his control of the ball under the most violent pressure was astonishing. The bewildering repertoire of feints and swerves . . . and balance that would have made Isaac Newton decide he might as well have eaten the apple.'

Hugh McIlvanney, *Belfast Telegraph*, 2004

*Edited excerpt from interview with George Best (*Parkinson in Australia, 1983)

GEORGE: You know, I'm the first to admit I was born with something a little bit special. And, even from early days, the manager of the club at the time told all the rest of the coaching staff to leave me alone and let me develop naturally, and that's exactly what happened.

MICHAEL: When you were a kid, though, how soon was it, how early on, that you realised you'd got this special talent?

GEORGE: Well, even when I was playing with the kids in Belfast – you know, where I was born. Up to fifteen, I was always the one that scored the goals in the team. So I was always a little bit better than the other kids. But not so much better. And when I went to Manchester United at fifteen, I didn't feel anything special until I got in the first team and played my first professional game at seventeen. And what I found out was that I could go out and do exactly the same thing I'd always been doing since I was a kid, and found it just as easy, even against players who'd been playing for years and years. I think that's when I realised there was something a little bit special.

MICHAEL: When you were a kid in Belfast – you came from this rough working-class area of Belfast – did you want to be a star? Do you want to be a star?

GEORGE: I don't think so, no. I actually took an examination to become a printer. And you know, my father – Belfast had such a big problem with unemployment – my father looked at something that he thought had a lasting future.

MICHAEL: A proper job.

GEORGE: A proper job, yes. [AUDIENCE LAUGHTER] Instead of standing on street corners. And then the chance came along at fifteen to go. I never dreamt that at fifteen it would happen. It virtually happened overnight, you know. Before I was twenty-one, I'd done almost everything in football.

MICHAEL: You'd done almost everything in life as well by the time you were twenty-one. [AUDIENCE LAUGHTER]

GEORGE: Almost, almost.

Let's celebrate the player that was George Best. The circus that surrounded him, and his battles to come to terms with it, we'll deal with later. As Sir Matt said to me when I was interviewing him for the 1975 biography of George, 'We had our problems with the wee fella, but I prefer to remember his genius.'

'Genius' is a word bandied around like confetti nowadays, but it is a word and a description that hangs lightly on those slim shoulders. He was the greatest player I have ever seen. When he was in his pomp he was sublime and unstoppable. But don't take my word for it, listen to men who really knew what they were talking about, what they were witnessing, what they were playing with. Again for the 1975 biography, among the people I talked to were George's friend and onfield minder Paddy Crerand, the great Sir Matt and Danny Blanchflower, who after leaving Aston Villa had become the heartbeat of the wonderful Spurs side that won the Double in 1961 playing football with a style that impressed and inspired Sir Matt. I asked them to give me their thoughts on George the player.

First Paddy: 'You could see in that game the complete range of his skills. That is what made him so special, his range. He could do more things better than any player I have ever seen. He was a magnificent distributor of a ball,

he could beat a man on either side using methods that
no one had ever thought about, he could shoot, he could
tackle, he was competitive and yet cool under pressure.

'What more could you want? I mean what is the perfect
player? Two good feet? The kid had them. Strong in the
air? He could beat men twice his size. Ability to score
goals? Only Greavesy and Law have equalled him and I
think his ability to score a goal out of nothing was even
greater than theirs. Courage? I've never seen a braver player.
He could play at the back, in midfield or anywhere up
front. He was probably the best bloody keeper at the club
too, but we never tried him.'

This is how Sir Matt assessed his skills: 'George Best was
gifted with more individual ability than I have ever seen
in any other player, certainly unique in the number of gifts.
He remained deceptively skinny-looking but he was strong
and courageous to a degree that compensated amply. He
had more ways of beating a player than any other player
I have ever seen. Every aspect of ball control was perfectly
natural to him from the start. He even used his opponents'
shins to his advantage by hitting the ball on to them so
accurately that it came back to him like a one–two pass.

'He had more confidence in his ability than I have ever
seen in any other sportsman. He was always able to use

George in his pomp – sublime and unstoppable.

either foot (sometimes he seemed to have six!). His heading was devastating. If he had a fault in those younger days it was that he wanted to beat too many opponents when he could have passed the ball to better advantage. You could see him beat two or three or even four and then lose the ball and you would be having apoplectic fits and saying to yourself, "Why the hell don't you pass the ball more?" Then he would beat four men and score the winner. What do you do about that?'

I asked Danny Blanchflower to place in order of preference Stanley Matthews, Tom Finney and Best. Danny voted for George. Why? I wondered.

'Stanley was a supreme dribbler who would fox even the most ruthless, sophisticated defences. But he was primarily a provider. Finney was perhaps a better all-rounder than Matthews. He could play anywhere in the forward line and besides that was a free goal scorer. But George Best gets my vote. A master of control and manipulation, he is also a superb combination of creator and finisher, he can play anywhere along the line.

'But more than the others he seems to have a wider, more appreciative eye for any situation. He seldom passes to a colleague in a poor position. He is prepared to carry the responsibility himself.

'But basically Best makes a greater appeal to the senses than the other two. His movements are quicker, lighter, more balletic. He offers the greater surprise to the mind and the eye. Though you could do nothing about it, you usually knew how Matthews would beat you. In those terms he was more predictable to the audience. Best has the more refined, unexpected range. And with it all is his utter disregard of physical danger.'

In an interview with the *Observer* in 1992, even the most successful and longest-serving Manchester United manager, Sir Alex Ferguson, a man not easily impressed

George was a target for every team's 'enforcer'.

or of many words, was akin to a gushing teenager in the first flush of love: 'George was unique, the greatest talent our football ever produced – easily! Here at Old Trafford they reckon Bestie had double-jointed ankles. Seriously, it was a physical thing, an extreme flexibility there. You remember how he could do those 180-degree turns without going through a half-circle, simply by swivelling on his ankles. As well as devastating defenders, that helped him to avoid injuries because he was never really stationary for opponents to hurt him. He was always riding or spinning away from things.'

But the God-given talent and freakish physical gifts were only half the story. He did not arrive on Earth the complete player; he made himself one. In George's opinion no one taught him how to play. How could they? He played football as if instructed by a higher power; no earthly advice could help him. When Sir Matt was delivering his pre-match tactical team talk he'd send George from the room and then instruct the remaining players to 'just give the ball to George'.

What George in his prime had in spades was an appetite for the game second to none. He ate, lived and breathed football. He was a student of the game as well as an assiduous trainer. His inspirations were the greats of that coruscating Real Madrid side who won five successive European Cups under the brilliant leadership of Di Stéfano and the quicksilver, mercurial talent of Francisco Gento. Whatever he saw them do he added to his repertoire. He wanted simply to be the best in the world and he worked harder than anyone else to try and achieve it. He wasn't born with two good feet but he worked so hard on it that he forgot which one was his natural foot. He worked on his heading, his finishing, his tackling, to the point where he became the complete player, and as Paddy Crerand pointed out, the best player in any position in the club except for goalkeeper, which he probably was as well, but nobody had the courage to tell Harry Gregg because Sir Matt would have ended up two players short the following week, with Harry Gregg on a murder charge.

What also shone through was George's pure joy at playing the game, revelling in his opportunity to display the full panoply of his gifts. He approached a game like a matador; Old Trafford was his bull-ring, his team-mates the picadors, the opposition the hapless toro bravo. He had a hatful of party pieces. He would stop mid-dribble and take off one boot, then use his stockinged feet to pass to a team-mate. He'd strip off his shirt and wave it over

Team-mates didn't always appreciate George's love of showboating.

his head like a rodeo performer. On one memorable occasion I was invited with a group of his friends to watch him play at Old Trafford against Newcastle. It was a dull affair, so to spice things up, when he received a ball from the goalkeeper he ran over to the touchline below where his guests were sitting. He stood with his foot on the ball, waving at us, waiting for the Newcastle defenders. They arrived like a pack of wolves, scenting the blood of a cornered prey. But like his favourite comic book hero Zorro he disappeared in a flash, one bound and George was free – three wall passes off their legs, the ball chipped over their heads, the retrieval of the ball and then a theatrical bow to his dumbstruck and laughing guests.

Never was a man more certain of his ability, more in love with his talent. It was thrilling and unlike anything that had been seen on an English football field before. This love of showboating often led him into trouble with his team-mates, who would spend most of their training sessions being nutmegged and used as a piece of furniture for wall passes, and then Saturday afternoon running into support positions only to watch Best indulging in another piece of footballing fantasy.

In my interview with Sir Bobby, he remembers just such an episode more fondly than perhaps he felt at the time.

Edited excerpt from interview with Sir Bobby Charlton
(Parkinson, *2007*)

BOBBY: And then this little lad George Best came onto the scene. The coaches had been saying, 'Bobby, there's a really good young lad, a great young player in the juniors, he's just coming through, a little lad from Belfast.' And I thought, 'Well, they're laying it on a bit thick, nobody can be as good as that'. Then he came on the field and he played on the left wing against a friend of mine, a lad who played for Burnley, right back, John Angus, and he humiliated him. You know, this little lad was so brave and he was so tough – and his control! He did things that people were so excited about. And . . . I used to sometimes think he was a little bit selfish. [AUDIENCE LAUGHTER]

MICHAEL: He was.

BOBBY: Well, he was, he was. I mean, I don't know, Michael, if you remember, but Sir Matt Busby's assistant was Jimmy Murphy.

MICHAEL: Yes.

BOBBY: Who was the Welsh manager. And when I was fifteen and I first arrived at Old Trafford, he said, 'Bobby, you're now a professional, you can't play for yourself any more. If one of your players gets the ball, you have to give yourself, give him the option to pass to you. Make it easy for him. It's a team game this, not an individual game.' And

I remembered this through the whole of my early career. So when I got to George, George would pick the ball up, and my instincts would tell me, 'Go and help him. Go and make yourself available.' And I used to do this – and then George would look at me and go in another direction completely. [AUDIENCE LAUGHTER]

I got to the stage when I promised myself the luxury of not falling for it again. I'm at the edge of the 18-yard box, and George picks the ball up. We're playing Nottingham Forest and they have a little full-back called Joe Wilson playing for them. And Joe's trying to kick him and get him, and George starts weaving and dribbling, with the ball apparently tied to his shoelaces. And I'm standing there and my instincts are wanting to go to help him. But then I looked at the clock, and there was two minutes to go, and we were three up. And I thought, 'No, George, you've used me enough.' [AUDIENCE LAUGHTER] 'I'm not going to fall for it any more.' And I'm saying to myself, 'Don't you go, don't you go. Stand still, stand still.' And George starts weaving and dribbling. And I'm saying, 'Stand still, don't you go near him.' And George goes across the field and eventually hits the touchline on the other side and weaves his way back. And I'm saying, 'Stand still, stand still, don't you go near him. We're all right here with the score.' And then he turned in again, and it came so close to me, I couldn't resist it. And I said, 'George, you greedy little . . . What a fantastic goal that was!'

All these observations have to be understood within the context of the way the game was played in the 1960s. Busby had already recognised that football was becoming more robotic, with teams trying to work out how to stop players rather than overcoming them with superior skill and collective teamwork. Moreover, football back then was an intensely physical game, with players offered little protection. Defenders were given carte blanche to kick opponents, safe in the knowledge that the ref would do little more than wag his finger at them, even if the transgression would have ended in the law courts if it had been committed in a town centre at chucking-out time.

Every team had at least one enforcer, one hard man. There was Peter Storey at Highbury, Ron 'Chopper' Harris ruled the Bridge, Tommy Smith made Anfield a house of horrors and Leeds were 'blessed' with the unholy trinity of Norman Hunter, Jackie Charlton and Billy Bremner, who would kick you between them like a pinball, and if they were feeling off colour then there was always Johnny Giles and Paul Reaney. It was not a game for the faint-hearted. Nor, if you were five foot eight inches and nine stone wringing wet, was it a good idea to draw attention to yourself by making any of these or their team-mates look a fool. But that was exactly what George did and he loved every minute of it. Sometimes they caught him. I remember him coming off the pitch after one match with the backs of his legs covered with stud marks and bruises in all shades of green and purple from the kicking that had been administered, but for the most part his balance, two-footedness, speed and stamina left these monsters flailing in his wake.

This combination of talent, footballing nous, physical bravery and sheer hard work meant that by the time he made his debut in 1963 he was equipped to overcome any physical, mental or tactical challenge that was thrown at him. He was fitter, on a different plane skill-wise and quicker in mind and body than all those who played with and against him.

I remember his debut game. It was in 1963 against West Bromwich Albion at Old Trafford. He was opposed by a nuggety Welsh international full-back called Graham Williams who was intent upon taking this scrawny youth with too much hair and a big reputation down a peg or two. Best took him on and even nutmegged him, which in those day was the equivalent of signing his own death warrant. It also convinced Matt Busby to switch him to the other wing for the second half, ensuring that George's career was extended beyond one game. Sir Matt told me later that what struck him most about Best was his calmness before that game. While others prowled, smoked or indulged in pre-game superstitious rituals, this young lad sat cross-legged in the corner and looked for all the world as if he was waiting for a bus. When he went out and played he looked like someone playing their 300th game and not their first. It was a game George would always hold special because it was one he had been preparing for all his life.

As a lovely coda to that memory, I was present when some years later outside Stamford Bridge George met Graham Williams again. Graham asked George to stand still so he could study his face. 'Why?' asked George. 'Well, I want to know what you really look like, because all I've ever seen of you is your arse disappearing down the touchline.'

That period when George ruled Old Trafford was magical and at times the football he played beggared belief, while many of his performances were irresistible. Like a butterfly emerging into the sunlight, Best revealed the full beauty and potency of his game at Stamford Bridge in September 1964. His single-handed demolition of Chelsea saw him applauded off the field by both sets of fans after the 2–0 victory, whilst Ken Shellito, the opposition full-back turned inside out by Best, had been forced to leave the field with what Paddy Crerand called a serious case of 'twisted blood'.

With Best established in the side, Busby now had the final piece of the jigsaw he had been piecing together since Munich. Busby had already bought Denis Law from Torino for the then princely sum of £115,000 and spent a further £200,000 on other players, crucially including Paddy Crerand. All he needed was one more ingredient, another Duncan Edwards who could do it all better than anyone else, and along came Best.

So, armed with the potent but complementary talents of the Holy Trinity of Law, Charlton and Best, allied to Paddy's intelligent probing and robust marshalling from midfield, aided and abetted by a little lad called Nobby Stiles, who had the look and pallor of an undertaker's clerk yet would snap at the heels of the opposition's playmaker like a hyperactive terrier whilst gently persuading anyone who decided they might like a piece of George that it wasn't going to happen on his watch, Busby could start to dream of European glory and avenging the ghosts of Munich.

One balmy night in Lisbon in 1966 brought that dream one step closer to reality and changed for ever the life of George Best: Benfica away in the second leg of their European Cup quarter-final. United had narrowly won the first leg 3–2 and no one gave them a chance – Benfica in the bearpit of the Estádio da Luz, with the great Eusébio pulling the strings. Lambs to the slaughter. Busby thought the sensible approach would be to try and keep them quiet for the first twenty minutes, get their crowd on their backs. Eminently sensible, yet George had other ideas. He went out and destroyed Benfica, scoring two goals in the first twelve minutes and inspiring a magnificent 5–1 victory, whilst Busby watched helpless from the sidelines with exasperated admiration.

They didn't win the cup that year, but Busby now knew he could. For Best there was no turning back. He was now an international star. Coming back from Lisbon, he stuck a sombrero on his head and he was featured for different reasons on both the front and back cover of the *Daily Mirror*. The sports pages lauded his genius; the front page christened him the Fifth Beatle, a new star with the looks and the talent to be rated alongside Lennon, McCartney, Starr and Harrison, who were at the same time taking the pop world by storm and stealing the hearts

Hold the front page – George returns in triumph from Lisbon in 1967.

of teenage girls. That skinny, homesick, cripplingly shy fifteen-year-old apprentice now stood at the summit of the footballing world and had become a sex symbol.

'I was the one who took football off the back pages and put it on page one.'

George Best

Best's impact on the game of football went far beyond his feats on the pitch. A few years before George played for Manchester United, the maximum wage for a professional footballer was set at £20 a week. Footballers were ordinary working men, who dressed the same as their fans, lived in similar houses in similar streets to them. You could meet them in the billiard halls and travel to the game on the same bus as them. Stadiums were filled with cloth caps, and players played with a sensible haircut held in place by a good dose of brilliantine.

Until Jimmy Hill bravely stuck his chin above the parapet and won a fight to abolish the maximum wage in 1961, most footballers had second jobs and little job security. Even after the revolution inspired by Hill there was little that was glamorous about football or footballers. Sure, there was the odd Jaguar being bought, the nice semi-detached in a leafy suburb. Footballers became middle-class and could afford the odd night out and drink in a trendy club, but they were for the most part solid, family men, their virtues and attitudes still firmly stuck in the 1950s.

George changed the way football and footballers were viewed. His talent, looks and desire to entertain changed the palette of the inside of stadiums here and abroad from drab sepia to vivid colour. The terraces had a soprano section for the first time and the image and potential earning power of a footballer were transformed. He gave football glamour and a lot more besides. He grew his hair long, sported a beard and transformed the acceptable image of a sportsman from the conventional clean-shaven, short-back-and-sides look. He played football but dressed like a pop star.

Other players followed suit and suddenly football became a branch of entertainment, footballers became fashion icons and the earning potential of every player rose exponentially. George Best created the footballer as a brand. He made them attractive to companies and products way beyond the staple endorsements such as shin pads and other pieces of kit. George made it possible for footballers to promote goods that had little to do with the sport and which cut across every age and social class.

He was for football and the footballers to come a game-changer on and off the pitch. For George, it was a journey that began with an ambition to simply play professional football the way he knew he could, but ended up as a solo trek into an unknown world of fame and fortune for which there was no map, while everyone else stayed behind and wondered at what the hell he was doing, powerless to help.

In three short years, he had become the Fifth Beatle, a world star and a sex symbol. He was probably entitled to ask, how did that happen?

Chapter 5

MANCHESTER

'If I'd have been born ugly, you would never have heard of Pelé.'

George Best

In digs with Mrs Fullaway, one of the few points of stability in George's life.

Edited excerpt from interview with George Best
(Parkinson *in Australia, 1983)*

MICHAEL: I remember at Manchester United in those days, there'd be fifty thousand people watching you, and there was that baritone of sound. But when *you* walked onto the field, the soprano section started.

GEORGE: Mmm. [AUDIENCE LAUGHTER]

MICHAEL: About ten thousand girls, who didn't know one end of a football field from the other.

GEORGE: Yeah. It really was. You know, it was the Swinging Sixties in England, particularly in the north of England where the team was from. It was the time of the Beatles and the Rolling Stones, and I became sort of part of it, really.

MICHAEL: You did.

GEORGE: It was frightening, you know. When I look back, it was frightening. Seventeen, eighteen, I had my own fan club. I was receiving anything up to five thousand letters a week from all over the world. And as you say, most of them from young girls, who were treating me like a pop star. It really was a frightening experience, looking back. It was enjoyable too: I was the same as everybody, I loved to see my name in the paper.

If Munich inadvertently sealed George Best's fate and Sir Matt made United the perfect fit, the icon that was George Best was forged in Manchester. It was also the town in which I met George for the first time, as I began my career in television. It was an important and transformative place for both of us.

Amongst all this modern-day white noise full of buzzwords from Whitehall mandarins about creating 'Northern Powerhouses', there is a simple fact that the highly educated simpletons who for the most part run our country seem to have missed, or perhaps it wasn't included in their Classics lessons. The North has always been full of powerhouses, and none more so than Manchester. Moreover, it managed to become one, on numerous occasions and for different reasons, all by itself. It was the world centre of cotton production and a boom town in the Industrial Revolution, our first industrialised city. It was here that Marx met Engels, and the rest, as they say, is dialectical history, and if you want any more evidence that Manchester has always been a powerhouse, then I bet you didn't know that it was here, in 1909, that Ernest Rutherford split the atom. So there, stick that in your 'Northern Powerhouse' pipe.

Post-war was a grim time for Manchester, exacerbated by the rapid de-industrialisation of the British economy, particularly in the North, as well as the lack of any discernible plan to reinvigorate those places upon which the wealth and world power of Great Britain had been built. The North and its once-great towns became desolate, depressing places but, as ever, they refused to be laid low. Manchester in particular rose again in a most unexpected manner.

If the Fifties were monochrome, the Sixties were technicolor. If the Fifties were about moderation and rationing, the Sixties were about excess. If the Fifties were about propriety, the Sixties were about free love. If the Fifties were about respect for authority, then the Sixties were a V-sign to anyone over forty in a pinstripe suit. It was an exciting time to be young and British. It was even more exciting to be young and from Manchester.

The Sixties were the result of a spontaneous combustion caused by the confluence of a number of political, technological, social and cultural influences that came together in the first part of that decade. But the spark that lit the fuse was youth.

The young in the Sixties were the first for two generations not to face conscription. Their parents had fought in a world war and wanted their children to have the freedom to enjoy their youth. This generation would be radically different from their parents. The 'white heat of technology' had fundamentally changed the way people worked, giving them more free time and more money, while labour-saving devices in the home meant that women could remove the shackles of labour-intensive domestic chores. Televisions and transistor radios shrank the world and brought new music, new fashions and new ideas to this hungry, enquiring mass of young men and women. The world thrummed with anti-war protests, feminist ideas. England won the World Cup and America aimed to put a man on the Moon – for the first time in a long while everything seemed possible. As a result, the world was filled with a heady optimism. Everyone went on a spending spree of mass consumerism, sex came out from under the covers, and the trestles of the old order, if not kicked over, were certainly given a good boot.

I was lucky to be there at the moment that brief, hysterical, cultural revolution took off. I was working as a producer on a programme called *Scene at 6.30* for the newly formed Granada Television in Manchester. It was a magazine programme that had a music slot which was more often than not filled by our resident band, made up of four young men from Liverpool, called the Beatles. One day, John Lennon said that they were off to London the following morning to record a song they'd just written called 'Love Me Do'. The next time they came to Manchester, 10,000 screaming girls chased them down Cross Street and Britain in the Sixties took off.

I always maintain that the epicentre of the Cultural Revolution in the Sixties was Manchester. In my opinion, if you weren't in Manchester in the Sixties, then you weren't in the Sixties. London was Carnaby Street, flares, frocks and miniskirts worn by a waif from Neasden with an androgynous sex appeal called Twiggy. The soundtrack to that time might have been provided by the Beatles, but Manchester was the cultural heart, with George Best as its physical incarnation. No one was more suited to the role; it was like he had been born to do it. He was impossibly good-looking, anti-authoritarian and didn't see the need to conform in either his private or public life. He was the poster boy of the movement that was sweeping the youth of the land. He became the Pied Piper of Sixties Britain.

Wherever George went, others followed; whatever he wore set the fashion; how he cut his hair set the trend; if he sported a beard, everyone threw away their razors. He lived his life how he wanted and they loved him for it. He became much more than a footballer: he became a cultural icon attracting column inches from commentators on social affairs rather than sport. He appeared in the broadsheets as well as tabloids. Around him Manchester bloomed into life, its grimy patina washed away in a flood of boutiques, nightclubs, bars and hairdressing salons. The streets were full of girls in miniskirts and men with long hair. The night was theirs and there was a real possibility they'd end up in bed together.

But what turned it into something more than sex, drugs and Georgie Best was the presence of Granada Television, which grew to become one of the defining cultural forces of the Sixties. Its creator, Sidney Bernstein, was certain that his independent franchise should be up North. He said in 1954, 'Granada preferred the North because of its tradition of home-grown culture, and because it offered a chance to start a new creative industry away from the metropolitan atmosphere of London . . . the North is a closely knit, indigenous, industrial society; a homogeneous cultural group with a good record for music, theatre, literature and newspapers, not found elsewhere in this island.'

I was lucky to be in on the ground floor of that enterprise. This was a very important period of my life, the start of my career in television. I'd left Fleet Street under something of a cloud and was called up one day by a friend called Barrie Heads, who I had worked with at the *Yorkshire Post*, and asked if I fancied a job as a producer in television. I told him I didn't know how to produce television and he said, 'Don't worry, neither do the rest of us.' So that was that. The wet-behind-the-ears pioneers rolled into Quay Street, Manchester, and set up what the head of the station, David Plowright, described as 'the most innovative, self-opinionated, insufferably arrogant television company of the lot'.

Bernstein invented an area of Britain which he called Granadaland and it became a very potent force. People in the region used to have their channel selector knob permanently rusted to Granada Television's Channel 3. Bernstein was only half joking when he devised an April Fool's Day stunt in which anybody coming into

Granadaland had to have their passports stamped. Sidney Bernstein developed this strong sense of identity and a feeling that something really wonderful was happening – and it was.

Surrounded by the cream of British journalism, by young men like Leslie Woodhead and Michael Apted, who'd go on to shape and define British television and film for future generations, and urged on by Bernstein's insistence that in every office a picture of P.T. Barnum should be hung to remind us we must never forget the razzle-dazzle, I was part of a television company that created some of the most celebrated and ground-breaking television the UK had ever produced. Programmes like World in Action and Coronation Street which broke the mould and set new standards in editorial quality and longevity. And like moths to the flame, Northern actors like Tom Bell, Albert Finney and Tom Courtenay, writers like Jack Rosenthal, Alan Bennett, Keith Waterhouse, Willis Hall and Alan Plater, as well as pop groups and comics, all found their way to Quay Street.

The cultural and artistic centre of Britain relocated to Manchester and, for the first time, had a Northern voice and sensibility. Whereas before with my accent I couldn't get a job as a doorman at the BBC, now you had to have

Against a backdrop of worshipping fans, George Best cuts a wistful figure in this appealing and moving impressionist portrait.

The 'little lad from Belfast' in 1963. Manchester tingled with expectation that this footballer with the physique of a toothpick might be something special.

The terrier-like Nobby Stiles, left, did his best to protect George on the field, while Bobby Charlton, right, was often kept waiting for the pass that never came.

No tracksuit managers here. Sir Matt Busby in 1971, flanked by the 'Holy Trinity' of Bobby Charlton, Denis Law and George, left, and Brian Kidd, Paddy Crerand and David Sadler, right.

After Manchester United's victory in the 1968 European Cup, the personal award of the Ballon d'Or capped a life-changing season for George.

'The fact that I was so fit, I got away with a lot' – George and Denis Law put in the hard work in training.

In his Manchester boutique, George plays it cool as Lucy Farrington serenades him with her single 'Georgie' in 1970.

Quick in mind and body, George leaves World Cup winner Alan Ball trailing in his wake in 1969.

'They reckon Bestie had double-jointed ankles' – George evades the despairing tackle of Jim McCalliog of Wolves in 1971.

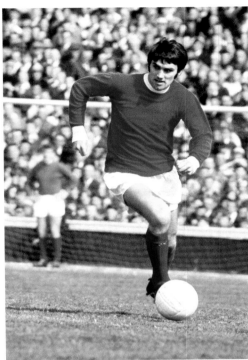

I know George would still have been a superstar in the era of Lionel Messi, above left, Cristiano Ronaldo, below left, and David Beckham, below right – but how would they have fared in his?

Thousands lined the route to Stormont as Belfast's favourite son received what amounted to a state funeral.

my accent to get a presenting job there. It was here, a few weeks after George broke into the Manchester United first team, that I conducted my first television interview. It was with a very polite and softly spoken young man called Mick Jagger. When I asked him how long he thought he would go on being in the Stones, he reckoned he was 'pretty well set up for another year'. It just went to prove that none of us really knew what was happening around us. It was a wonderful place to be. Granada made you part of the Manchester scene and I went along with it. Everything was interlocked – Granada Television, the showbiz scene, the members of which drank champagne with George at the bar of his Slack Alice nightclub or sometimes at the Brown Bull pub in Chapel Street near Granada Studios, which was the de facto green room for the cast of *Coronation Street* and a place where I was known to partake of a drink or two – but its centre was definitely Manchester United and George Best.

George was having a lovely time, totally unaware of his role in this cultural and social upheaval but taking full advantage of everything that was on offer. He had everything to live for, and when in 1968, at Wembley in the final of the European Cup, destiny called, he didn't go missing.

I was at the game. For the most part I was bored stiff. Stiles marked Eusébio out of the game, whilst Best was virtually anonymous, a mixture of tight marking and an unusually off-key performance by him. United were lucky to reach extra time, as Eusébio missed a great chance three minutes from the end of normal time. Alex Stepney's save was astonishing, but a player of Eusébio's class should have buried it.

The rest, as they say, is history. Stepney clears the ball upfield in the opening minutes of extra time. Brian Kidd flicks it on and Best picks it up, nutmegs the centre half, dummies the goalkeeper and rolls the ball into the net. He was tempted, he later told me, to walk the ball up to the line, kneel down and head it in, but with the Benfica defence steaming towards him, he thought he'd better not tempt the sporting gods too much. United were ahead and from that moment on Benfica crumbled.

Busby had fulfilled his last ambition. He could finally lay to rest the ghosts of Munich and put down that burden he had been carrying since that awful night ten years before. His new Duncan had delivered and was soon to be crowned the European Footballer of the Year. His new

Duncan remembered the game but little else. There was a reception, a banquet, but he had no recollection of the celebrations because he was drunk. He left the banquet early to spend the night with a girlfriend.

It was the moment when George Best's life began to go into freefall, when Bacchus replaced Busby. None of us knew it, none of us could see it, but at the height of his success and fame, our mate George was beginning to crumble. On a night when the possibilities for him and Manchester United seemed limitless, it was in fact the beginning of the end. We all continued to bask in the reflected glory of this beating heart of Manchester, but he was already on his way to the exit from the party he had helped create.

George ponders a life without football after retiring for the first time, in 1972.

Chapter 6

DECLINE AND FALL

'*I was born with a great gift and sometimes that comes with a destructive streak. Just as I wanted to outdo everyone when I played, I had to outdo everyone when we were out on the town.*'

George Best

IN January 1974, George Best left Old Trafford for the last time and turned his back on football and, although we didn't know it then, the world in general. His reason for finally leaving the club that had been his home since he was fifteen was being dropped by the new manager, Tommy Docherty, for a cup tie against Plymouth Argyle. Docherty had had enough of George's increasingly erratic behaviour, and George knew his time at Old Trafford was over. He sat in the empty stands after the match and tried to recall the golden moments of his reign as the King of Manchester, but he just felt empty and alone. From that point on George was lost to us.

After Manchester United he struggled to find a role and a life that satisfied him. He would still dabble in football, mainly for monetary reasons. There would be the occasional comeback in America or other outposts of the known world, plus a game here and there for teams as incongruous as Fulham, Hibernian and Stockport. Alongside this there would be the monumental drinking binges, broken relationships, business failures, all of it punctuated by attempts at drying out, repeated promises that he had changed and announcements that he had met the love of his life. He got married, had a child. But nothing worked. His life was chaotic, spinning out of control, with Bestie hanging on by his fingertips. Those who cared for him looked on with concern, unable to help, unable to reach him.

But the problems had begun a long time before that final parting from United. Even when times were good and George was loving his new-found celebrity status and all the trappings, financial and personal, that came with it, his life was beginning to unravel.

At the end of the previous chapter, I suggested that it was the night after his 1968 European Cup success that marked the start of the downturn of his life. However, interestingly, I once asked Matt Busby when he thought the rot set in. He reckoned it was even earlier. Matt believed, incredibly, that George's decline began after his stunning performance in Lisbon, in 1966. How remarkable that at the zenith of his power as a player and fame as a man he was already taking his first steps on the dark road he would follow for the rest of his life. It seems inexplicable, and yet I had seen something in George when I first met him that made me wonder.

I was a friend of George for over forty years and it was never dull. On the other hand, I suspect that his friends – or most of them I knew – had a better time than he did. As soon as we met, I instantly saw that there was within him a profound unhappiness and dissatisfaction with the world around him. It was a part of him that I first wrote about in my 1975 biography. Near the end of that book there is a passage that imagines a typical night out for George. I had talked to him at length and been on enough of these nights out, at least for part of them, to be fairly certain that my fantasy was firmly rooted in reality. It makes for uncomfortable and depressing reading. Little did I know that I was writing a blueprint for the rest of his life.

The curtains didn't quite meet in the middle and the sunlight illuminated the room. The young man in the bed opened his eyes and went through his morning routine.

First check the wallpaper. If you recognise it you're at home, if not you are playing away and the question is where? This time it is familiar. Home sweet home. Next, check the other side of the bed. He turned over slowly so that the girl next to him didn't wake up as he inspected her face. They always looked different in the morning. At least that's what he had been told. He didn't know because he never remembered what they looked like the night before. This one was young, slim, long blonde hair.

What happened?

Can't remember.

Not a bloody clue. She wakes up, looks at him for a minute, smiles. Nice teeth. 'Good morning, George.'

What's her bloody name?

'Good morning, love,' he says.

They all react to 'love'.

Next stage of routine.

Get rid.

'Well, love, I've got to go now because I've got training in an hour.'

'All right. Will I see you again?'

'Sure, give me a ring.'

'You must have thousands of girlfriends.'

'Millions.'

'I hope you don't think I just sleep with any guy.'

'Certainly not.'

'I hope that you don't think I slept with you just because you are George Best.'

'Never crossed my mind.'

'In fact I didn't know who you were till my mate told me.'

'Of course. Do you have a car?'

'You know I haven't got one. You drove me here.'

'I'll get a cab.'

'It was great last night, wasn't it?'

'Great.'

He wished he could remember. He rang a cab and returned as the girl dressed. Good figure. He really did wish he could remember. The cab came and she left. The driver gave him a leer as he kissed her good-bye on his doorstep.

'On my account,' said George.

'As usual,' said the driver.

He went back indoors and contemplated what to do. He didn't feel like training, he never did. Not recently anyhow. There was a time when he couldn't get enough of it, training, that is, but now it was getting more and more difficult to turn in. He rang one of his mates.

'Tell the club I can't make training today. Tell them I've got a cold,' he said.

He went back to bed, where he could still smell the girl. Wished he could remember what she had been like. And what was her name? Christ, he never did find out and so when she rang he wouldn't know who it was. She'd say, 'It's Anne here,' or some such name and he'd say, 'Are you the one with the long blonde hair?'

Messages.

Who'd phoned while he was out? He switched on the ansaphone. Two obscene calls, a message from his agent, his mum phoned and an interesting call from a party in London which he hadn't been able to get to. They'd rung him up and all the guests had recorded a message. 'Hello, darling Georgie,' said a lush feminine voice. 'Take me to bed and make love to me, Georgie boy,' she said. The message ended in giggles. He switched the machine off and went to sleep.

He woke up mid-afternoon and drove to his shop in the E-type. He had a white Rolls but the kids used to scratch their initials on it. Once they slashed the tyres. He drove to his shop in the city centre where the school-girls, legs like sparrows, pressed their noses to the window pane and swooned when he made an appearance. So long as he stayed in the shop, so long as they stood and stared.

'One day I'll throw their bloody peanuts back at them,' he said.

Two Manchester urchins, raggy arsed and snotty nosed and braver than the female admirers, stuck their heads round the shop door.

'Georgie Best, Superstar
Walks like a woman
Doesn't wear a bra,'

they chanted.

'Piss off,' he said without malice.

Another kid came through the door and stared at him with grave child's eyes.

'What's your second name, mister?' he asked.

'Best.'

'No, that's what you are, but what do they call you?' said the kid.

'Bloody hell,' said George Best.

He was waiting for the pubs to open. He always went to the same one, had to really, no choice. New pubs meant bother, aggravation, some joker coming up and wanting to have a fight. He always went to the same pub and stood in the same corner with the same fellas. Before he went to the pub he made a phone call to a girl he'd met a week or so ago. A little darling. A woman answered the other end.

'Is Janice there?' he said.

'Who is it?' the woman said.

'Georgie,' he said.

'Georgie who?' she said.

'Georgie Porgie, pudding and pie, kissed the girls and made them cry,' he said.

'Don't get cheeky with me, I'm Janice's mother,' the woman said.

He knew she was, that was why he didn't tell her his name. He used to have this mental picture of some dear suburban mum, worried stiff about her beautiful daughter, getting a phone call from Georgie Best. With his reputation the mother would faint and when she woke up she'd lock her daughter in the coal shed before informing the police. That's why he said daft things on the phone when the mum asked the second name.

Back to Janice's mum.

'Sorry, missus,' he said. 'The name is George Smith.'

'How very unusual,' the woman said. 'I'll tell Janice you called.'

Long-time friend Malcolm 'Waggy' Warner applies the final touches for a TV commercial.

'Ta, missus,' he said.

That would be another girl who didn't get the message that he called. Never mind, a few drinks and then a good gamble, then a tour of the discos looking for girls. The night might burst into a thousand stars. The drinking is harmless really, and good fun. There's Waggy, the hair-dresser, and Big Frank, the builder, and Danny, the United nut case, all mates and have been for years and when they are around there's no trouble. That comes later when they've gone home like sensible people and he remains lurching from place to place, getting drunk and losing money.

He stood at the bar all night, never moving, just steadily drinking. One day one of his mates had said, 'Have you seen my imitation of George Best?' and he just stood in a corner with a drink in his hand saying nothing.

Very funny.

When the pubs closed he went gambling. As he went into the club an elderly couple were coming out. They looked like his granny and grandad.

'Good luck, George,' said the old lady.

'How have you done, love?' he asked.

'Got clattered, that's what,' her husband said.

'Got a reet bloody clattering toneet, that's what.'

'Mug's game, gambling,' said George.

'You can say that again,' said the old man.

The bouncer just inside the door must have weighed twenty stone. He had eyes like dried currants. 'Good evening, gentlemen,' he said without moving his lips.

'Can you do me a favour, George?' he said. George nodded. 'Little girl I knew fell down, broke her neck. Very sad. In hospital. Crippled. Would appreciate a visit from you. Thinks you're smashing. Just a minute to see her. Can you go? Do her the world of good.'

'I'll try,' said George.

The man's fat face crumpled into a smile. 'I'd very much appreciate it, George. And if there's anything I can do for you . . .' He placed a hand the size of a small shovel on the footballer's shoulder.

'He doesn't hit people, he just falls on them,' said George Best.

He went to the tables and started gambling with £10 chips.

The croupier said, 'Go home. I was having a good time till you came in.'

Around him the faces of the other gamblers were elated with concern or excitement or studied nonchalance. He just looked bored.

Big Nobby, a born loser, joined him.

'Would it make any difference if I used your money?' he said.

'No bloody chance,' said George who was winning.

'I'll just stand next to you then. It might rub off,' said Nobby.

'Likely,' said George and kept on winning.

'What am I doing here when I could be at home getting whipped?' said Nobby.

'Mug's game, gambling,' said George softly.

'It bloody is the way I play it. Do you realise you're winning what I'm losing and we're supposed to be mates?' said Nobby.

'I don't use any system,' said George, to no one in particular.

'I've got a great new system,' said Nobby. 'I pick up all the chips and sling 'em at the croupier and say "Fuck it".'

Another gambler sidled up to George. His wife was ill and would appreciate his autograph. He signed on a pound note.

'Thanks. Sorry about your troubles at United and the rest,' the man said.

'Don't worry, I'm not,' said George.

Nobby was broke.

'Do you take Mongolian traveller's cheques?' he asked the croupier, and sagged in his suit.

'I think I'll go and lie down in the road. With my luck I'd get swept up rather than run over,' he said.

George cashed his chips. He had about £600 in notes. He put them in a paper bag and carried the money away under his arm. It was past midnight.

He went into a discotheque and sat facing the door of the ladies' powder room. He always sat there because he had worked out that sooner or later every girl in the club went through that particular door and he didn't want to miss a single one. Some stared back at him, openly sexual and inviting, others pretended they'd not noticed. A few came and sat down and talked to him.

One said, 'Read in the paper you missed training today.'

He nodded.

'What's the matter?' she said.

'Can't get up,' he said.

'That's not what I heard,' she said, looking hard at him to make sure he understood the sexual innuendo.

He pretended not to understand.

'What I meant was I couldn't get out of bed,' he said.

'You don't have much bloody trouble getting into bed though, do you?' the girl said.

'I'm a virgin,' said George.

He left the club after an hour and after satisfying himself there wasn't any girl there he really fancied. He tried two more discotheques but it was a bad night. No one he fancied.

It was three in the morning now but he hadn't finished. With his paper bag full of money under his arm he walked to the car and drove to the outskirts of the city to a large Victorian house. He climbed the metal fire escape and knocked on a door. A peephole appeared, an eye inspected the caller and then the door creaked open.

Inside there were potted plants, antimacassars, deep comfortable sofas and a bar. Phyllis, the owner, a handsome woman of middle age, stood at the bar. George liked Phyllis and whenever he was troubled he went to talk to her. He sat at the bar and started drinking.

'Read about you not turning up today,' said a man at the bar.

'Didn't feel like it,' said George.

'You want your bloody head testing,' said the man.

'I did have it tested. The club sent me. The guy said I was sane. That's more than can be said for some people,' said George.

'It's still daft. Who am I going to watch if you don't play for United?' he said.

'Stockport,' said George.

His friend said to George, 'Do you remember that game, I don't know who you were playing, but you got the ball in your own half past one man, then another, then another, then you juggled the ball from one foot to the other and whacked it in the corner. Do you remember?'

'I did all that?' said George incredulously.

'You did. You bloody did,' the man said.

'Leave him alone. He doesn't want to talk about bloody football,' said the first man.

'Why not, he's a bloody footballer, isn't he?' said his friend.

'Well you make bloody raincoats, but we don't talk about making bloody raincoats all the bloody time, do we?' the first man said.

'But making raincoats is not the same as playing bloody football for United,' the raincoat manufacturer said.

'I don't mind talking about soccer,' George said.

'Watch your bloody language,' said Phyllis, moving in to separate George from his new friends.

She took him across the room and sat next to him on a settee.

'Fed up again?' she asked.

'Choked,' he said.

'It's a small town,' she said.

'A bloody village. Just like Peyton Place,' he said.

'Same anywhere, George love,' she said.

'I think I'll jack it in and go and live in Spain,' he said.

'You have to earn money,' she said.

'I can always earn money. Sell my bloody story to the newspapers for thousands of pounds, then sod off,' he said.

'Why don't you do what you do best of all, play football?' she said.

'Fed up with the bloody game. I'm with a bad side and I don't enjoy it,' he said.

'You can't go on like this, drinking and staying out and the like,' she said and moved off to assist the raincoat manufacturer who was having difficulty getting off his stool.

A pretty girl who had been drinking with another man at the bar came up to George.

'Take me home, George,' she said.

'What about your friend?' said George, indicating the man at the bar.

'He's not a friend, he's my husband and I'm bored by him,' she said.

'Go away. I don't feel like fighting tonight,' said George.

'Ring me then,' she said.

'Sure,' he said.

'Have you got a pen and paper?'

'Don't need one. I've trained my mind specially to remember ladies' phone numbers,' he said.

She told him and went back to her husband.

He didn't want to go home. Not back to that bloody house. More like a goldfish bowl than a home. Training tomorrow. Must turn in tomorrow otherwise he'd be in deep trouble again. It was getting harder. Once upon a time, and not too long ago, he could go out, get drunk, get laid and turn up for training next morning fresh as a daisy. Or just about. Not now though. Nowadays getting up was a big problem, and he simply didn't want to go and train.

George Best, superstar, failed first class. He got bored during the day so he drank, he was bored in the evening so he drank some more. Then he didn't want to go home because he couldn't sleep properly so he got drunk again. Just like tonight.

A night out with George Best.

Come and get drunk with a celebrity.

A magical mystery tour round the inside of his head.

What makes George Best tick?

He'd be interested to have your theory because he really doesn't know himself.

Once there was this girl in London he was staying with. A nice kid and for a while he loved her. Then one day he just had to get out and leave her and go away. He thought about writing a note explaining and when he sat down to write it he couldn't find the words because he didn't know why he was leaving. So he just wrote 'Nobody knows me' on a piece of paper and left it on the mantelpiece when he crept out that morning while she was still asleep.

From the outside, George's life looked like one long party.

And that was the gospel truth.

He did things at times he couldn't possibly explain.

Reasons bothered him.

Like tonight. What he had just gone through, the gambling, the drinking, the daft conversations, he had done every night for two years.

He was destroying himself by inches.

The only footballer who was seventy per cent proof.

He said goodnight to Phyllis and went outside. It was daylight. Children were on their way to school. He went to his car and two kids stopped and watched him driving away. He thought of what would happen when they got to school and told teacher, 'We saw George Best this morning.'

She'd say, 'Don't be daft. You must be imagining things.'

Little did she know.

Looking at it again, I think that the one person I really wanted to read this description of a desolate and desperate night out was George. If he did, he never told me and it certainly didn't bring him up short. If I wanted it to be a lightbulb moment, it didn't work. The electricity had been cut off. But then if he did read it, he would've done so with one eye on the clock, checking to see if the pubs were open. He was the least introspective man I have ever met. He would sidestep any difficult question about his drinking or behaviour with a joke. Even Matt Busby, a man he revered and loved like a second father, couldn't reach him. George was closed off from the rest of us, locked in his own world.

But it didn't stop me trying. If ever he was in trouble I would offer him a bed at my house. A double bed, of course, with one side occupied by a different leggy blonde model each time. George would always bring a football and preferred to play with my three sons and the family cat rather than put up with me trying to advise him.

One time he went to a nightclub and next morning at breakfast he asked me if I could take him to London. My wife Mary was making herself a cup of coffee when down the stairs from George's bedroom walked a pretty young woman wearing evening dress and smoking a Balkan Sobranie. George had brought her home from his night out but had omitted to tell us. She was a nice girl and offered to do the washing-up. Mary thought she might ruin her dress, so the girl, determined to impress, started tottering round the house on high heels doing the hoovering. It's an amusing tale, but also instructive.

Another disposable blonde, another quick escape, a refusal to face up to the consequences of his actions.

Another time I had a summer party and invited a few friends over, but when I told them I had George coming the guest list swelled to include the likes of Michael Caine and the actress Sarah Miles. I never felt so popular, but in reality they were all there for George. It was memorable for two reasons. Firstly, I nearly lost the cream of the British theatre and film industry when my lovely old wooden riverboat suddenly sprang a leak and all that the occupants had to bail out the rising flood were champagne flutes. When the rapidly sinking boat finally limped its way close to the landing stage Michael Caine leapt nimbly ashore, prompting Sarah Miles to declare in her best mockney, ''Ere, Caine, I thought you were a bleeding hero!' And secondly, as soon as he could, George took himself away from the adults, all of whom were desperate to talk to him, and went off again to play football with the boys. The cat had given up football by this stage; he had found that mice, or even shadows, were easier to catch than George with a ball at his feet.

The world and his wife had come to see George and he turned his face away. But it didn't stop me and others trying. We did talk for hours about his drinking and self-destructive behaviour and I tried to persuade him that there was more to life than he was seeing, and that the choices he was making would only lead him down the wrong road. I continued the conversation in the same vein when I interviewed him on five occasions for my show. But again, apart from on one occasion, I never felt that he was truly facing up to what he had become, or indeed that he truly wanted to change.

I first interviewed him in 1971 and I would be fascinated to know what he said, but the BBC in their infinite wisdom decided that the first series of *Parkinson* was not worth preserving. Consequently, alongside the likes of culturally insignificant guests such as John Lennon and Orson Welles, George was deleted. Probably to make room for a fascinating documentary about a Peruvian nose-flute player. The next occasion was in 1973, when he quit Manchester United for the first time, citing disillusionment with the game and disappointment at the way Manchester were failing to bring new blood into the team. I tried in vain to get him to properly explain why, at the peak of his powers, he had turned his back on football. For him, it was clear that the problems were caused by outside factors and not by what was inside him.

Edited excerpt from interview with George Best
(Parkinson, 1973)

MICHAEL: Are you really not ever going to play football again, George?

GEORGE: No. People keep asking me, saying you must come back, you're going to come back. I made a decision almost a year ago and I changed my mind then, but this time I won't.

MICHAEL: You won't. What makes you so certain?

GEORGE: I don't know. I made a mistake the last time. I should have, when I said I was going to quit, I should have stayed out of it. I came back and faced the same sort of problems.

MICHAEL: Yes.

GEORGE: So this time I don't want to face any more problems.

MICHAEL: But is it possible, George – and I've known you for a long time – I mean, is it possible – I don't believe it is, you see – for you to live without football?

GEORGE: Well, so far. I don't know how long it is since I've played. Three or four months, I think. And I haven't missed it.

MICHAEL: You haven't?

GEORGE: No, not in the slightest, no.

MICHAEL: Let's go back to the point where you took this decision to end your career. What really was the reason?

GEORGE: It was a mixture of lots of things. In the game and out of the game. I wasn't enjoying playing as much as I had done. I wasn't as fit as I should have been, because of . . . It was my own fault.

MICHAEL: Why was that? Your drinking?

GEORGE: General things. Yeah. Nightlife and drinking.

MICHAEL: Yes.

GEORGE: Too many late nights. I wasn't enjoying training as much.

MICHAEL: Yes.

GEORGE: Which I always had done.

MICHAEL: Yes.

GEORGE: Even if I had been having late nights, I'd always enjoyed the training part of it.

MICHAEL: Yes.

GEORGE: But even that was becoming like a job.

MICHAEL: Yes.

GEORGE: Which it never had been before.

MICHAEL: Yes. But what about the things in the game that got you down? What were they specifically?

GEORGE: Well, it was basically my own form, rather than the form of the team. I wasn't enjoying the coaching side of it. The training side of it. There was just this general thing around Manchester United at the time.

MICHAEL: But would it have been any different if you'd gone to any other club?

GEORGE: It might have been. But I wouldn't have let anyone take the chance on paying a lot of money for me, and gone to them, and then maybe done exactly the same things with them. Especially after they'd paid a quarter of a million pounds.

MICHAEL: But that's an interesting thing, because what you are really saying is that you can't guarantee your own conduct.

GEORGE: Exactly. Yeah.

MICHAEL: Really?

GEORGE: Well, I do things on the spur of the moment. Instead of sitting down and thinking about them. I tend to run off and try to think about them, sort them out, somewhere else. It's usually in a different country.

MICHAEL: Yes. But this time you've sorted it out. You've come to the conclusion no more soccer, finished.

GEORGE: Yeah, definitely.

MICHAEL: What about money, George? Because there was a point when you were earning a great deal of money. Now the income's dried up because it all depended on football. I read an article in the *People* last week which said you were broke. Is that true?

GEORGE: It's funny because I got a phone call at ten to eight in the morning in Acapulco about two weeks ago. I was staying at a beautiful villa with my own swimming pool, bar stools dead under the bar, refrigerator and everything.

Beautiful weather. And I got a phone call from New York, some newspaper phoning me, and they asked me if I was broke. So I said that of course I was. I'd been in Toronto and Los Angeles, San Francisco, back to Los Angeles, Acapulco, I was going to Palm Springs. I said of course I'm broke. I mean how ridiculous can you get? Who do they think is paying for it?

MICHAEL: So you are not broke?

GEORGE: Not at the moment. No.

MICHAEL: I mean, are you comfortably well off?

GEORGE: Reasonably. I'd played since I was seventeen.

MICHAEL: Yes.

GEORGE: Until recently. That's nine years. I was earning good money and I didn't spend it all. I'm not well off. I haven't got a lot of money, which is why I've got to work and make more.

MICHAEL: But the more you look at it, George, the more daft it becomes, you see. Because here you are, this extraordinary talent. You could have worked until you were thirty-two or thirty-three, thirty-four, something like that. And then retired. You would have made a fortune, man. And you just jack it all in.

GEORGE: I might make more now that I've jacked it in.

[AUDIENCE LAUGHTER]

MICHAEL: But, you know, I hope you do, but I don't think so. The sad thing is that you deny us the pleasure of watching you play. You have no regrets about that at all? Do you have no instinct as an entertainer, which you've always said you were? Do you have no loyalty towards the audience?

GEORGE: A lot of people have asked me that, have said, 'Don't you think you owe the public something?' I'm not sure if I do or not. I'd like to think I've given them something for nine years. But I just couldn't take what was going on outside of the game. People say, 'Well, how can you have pressure and strains when you're doing something you're getting well paid for?' Which I don't think we do. You're training, you're keeping fit. But I think to be a British footballer, to play sixty-five/seventy games a year, sometimes two and three times a week, and at the end of it look forward to, what, three or four weeks' holiday? And you've also got to do what you're told, really.

MICHAEL: Yes.

GEORGE: For eleven months of the year.

MICHAEL: Yes.

GEORGE: You can't go and sort of go mad. You've got to be in bed at a reasonable hour and you can't relax completely. I think there's a hell of a lot of strain on professional footballers. When I first got into trouble, when they first started talking about me being under pressure and strain, at the same time there were three or four other First Division players who were having troubles. And if they had been single, as I was, and not married men with responsibilities, I think they would have done exactly the same as I did.

MICHAEL: Yes. Why don't you get married?

GEORGE: I can't afford it.

MICHAEL: But I mean really, a serious question. You are, what, twenty-seven now, aren't you?

GEORGE: Twenty-six.

MICHAEL: Twenty-six. You've been out with more girls than I've had hot dinners. [AUDIENCE LAUGHTER] Considerably more. Have you never found anybody that you wanted to marry?

GEORGE: Not really, no. If I had've done, I would have been very pleased because I love children. I love kids, and I'd have been the happiest man in the world if I could have found someone. But it just hasn't happened. I've taken a lot of girls out and if I'd have met the right one, I would have married her. But I just haven't.

MICHAEL: But what's the problem? Is it that they are after Georgie Best the superstar, rather than Georgie Best, ordinary Joe? Is that the problem?

GEORGE: No, I don't think so. It's pretty easy to spot the ones who are after you for your name. Well, I like to think I can. It's only common sense. So I don't know what it is, really. Maybe I'm too hard to please.

MICHAEL: Yes, yes. Are you going to go on looking?

GEORGE: Of course, yes.

MICHAEL: You talked earlier about the pressures within the game which you objected to. Would one of those pressures be that the game is getting dirtier? That people were kicking you more? That play was getting too hard?

GEORGE: I don't think it was getting dirtier. I think the game was becoming less enjoyable in Britain. I think generally the game was becoming a lot more boring to watch.

MICHAEL: Yes.

GEORGE: Games I've watched in other countries, they've been tremendous to watch. To watch Brazil or the West Germans, when they're really on song, and then to watch British football, there's just something missing. I don't know what it is. Maybe it's too much discipline. Too much method. I don't know. What is it?

MICHAEL: It will never get better, so long as players like you leave it, of course. That's the problem with it, you know. I mean, it's absolutely true: there is a lack of individuality in the game, which makes your retirement from it all the sadder. But tell me about the pressures outside of the game that you mention, that you didn't really go into. One reads stories about you being involved in punch-ups in pubs and all this kind of thing. To be honest, George, is a lot of it your fault?

GEORGE: I don't go into pubs and walk up to people and ask them if they want a fight. Probably, that's what people think I do. I used to. I've always had that. If I walk into a bar or a club, it happens all the time. You know there's always someone wants to come up and hit you over the head with a pint pot, and then go to work on a Monday morning and tell their mates. I used to put up with it, but I started to think, 'If they're going to walk up and threaten you, if you smack them in the mouth first, they're not going to go and tell their mates they sorted you out, if they've got a black eye and a bloody nose, are they?'

MICHAEL: Yes. But this was a real problem, was it?

GEORGE: It was. It happened everywhere. I've been hit over the head by a 65-year-old woman!

MICHAEL: Really?

GEORGE: In a club. Sitting watching a show, and she walked up and hit me over the head with her handbag.

MICHAEL: Why?

GEORGE: You tell me. [AUDIENCE LAUGHTER] Maybe she wasn't enjoying the show. I don't know.

MICHAEL: Did you enjoy being a superstar at all?

GEORGE: I did at first. I built my own image up first of all.

MICHAEL: You did.

GEORGE: And then I was horrified by it, when I was twenty-two, twenty-three. I mean, just to go anywhere at night, sit and watch a show and try and have an enjoyable evening, and 99 per cent of the time know that when you come out, someone's going to have slashed your tyres or gone round your car with a six-inch stiletto heel.

MICHAEL: Really?

GEORGE: It's pretty hard to sit and relax.

MICHAEL: Yes. But other people have gone through this and have survived it, George. I wonder what it is about you that's made you chuck it in.

GEORGE: Well, maybe I just didn't want to put up with it. Maybe other people were willing to put up with it and I wasn't. And I could afford not to put up with it.

MICHAEL: Yes.

GEORGE: And this last two or three months I don't think I've ever been as relaxed as I am.

MICHAEL: You're feeling good, are you?

GEORGE: Yes, I feel good.

MICHAEL: Really? Do you think, George, that you've got a future in this country? Because it's all very well saying you're out of football now, but you're not really out of the limelight at all, are you? Wherever you go, you're recognised, and I suppose there's some pressure on you to that extent. Are you going to stay here?

GEORGE: Yes, well, that will probably be a problem. I don't know how long it will last, maybe two, three years. So what I'm doing, if the businesses don't go well, the ones I'm planning on starting in England, then I'll try somewhere else. I'll maybe try it in America.

*

Once again in 1975, when I interviewed George to tie in with the publication of the biography, I tried to get him to explain the end of his love affair with Manchester and football in general. But he was again certain that he had left football for ever. A year earlier he had returned to Manchester United but had found the experience frustrating and claustrophobic, not helped by a fractious relationship with the new manager, Tommy Docherty. The problems he identified in the first interview were still there, still rankling him, and more importantly George hadn't changed. Indeed, he saw no need for himself to change. It wasn't his fault that he missed training to go on a binge; it was the rest of them. It was, in truth, a bad idea for him to try and return. His mind and body weren't in it or up to it. It was doomed from the start, no matter how many promises, on either side, were made.

Edited excerpt from interview with George Best (Parkinson, *1975)*

MICHAEL: I said in the introduction there's been a lot of speculation about you and your future. You're a free agent now, you've been given a free transfer by Manchester United. You can go where you want. What are you going to do?

GEORGE: I don't know. I have made up my mind that the first thing I want to do is just get myself as fit as possible. There's been a lot of offers coming in. But I've told everyone the same: I just want to get fit first. And then, when I feel I'm ready, I'll sit down and decide where to go.

MICHAEL: How many offers have you had from English First Division clubs?

GEORGE: So far, there's been five clubs on. And I've done the same, I've spoken to them and told them exactly the situation. I've said, let me get fit first. And when I've decided, I'll let you know.

MICHAEL: What kind of money are they offering, though? What's the highest offer you've had from an English First Division club?

GEORGE: I've been offered, as a signing-on fee, sixty thousand pounds from one club.

MICHAEL: Sixty thousand. That would pay the rent for a week or two, wouldn't it? [AUDIENCE LAUGHTER]

GEORGE: A few vodkas.

MICHAEL: Yeah, right. You've also been associating, I know, with American football clubs. There's been a lot of interest over there. What kind of money are we talking about?

GEORGE: Well, as you know, the Americans are trying to sell the game. And as you probably know, Pelé's over there. Eusébio's been there. And they're talking – over a period of, say, three or four seasons – a minimum of a million dollars.

MICHAEL: That's a signing-on fee and a contract for playing football?

GEORGE: That's just the football part of it. And then, of course, there's the commercial side, which could be anything. I'd be crazy not to think about it, because it's a hell of a lot of money.

MICHAEL: That's the most tempting offer you've had so far, I would imagine, to go to America.

GEORGE: It is. To be quite honest, I think I'll go to America.

MICHAEL: You do?

GEORGE: Yes.

MICHAEL: Just purely for the money? Or because there's something wrong, you think, with English football that doesn't attract you any more?

GEORGE: I think it's a mixture. When Manchester United gave me a free transfer, it all started again. The press were on, and last week for instance a few newspapers said things that weren't very complimentary to me. And I thought, 'Why the hell should I stay here and go through all that again?'

MICHAEL: Yes.

GEORGE: When I can go to America and earn twenty times as much as I can earn here.

MICHAEL: Yes.

GEORGE: And not get crucified for doing it.

MICHAEL: The press apart, and we'll come back to that later, what is it that is so unattractive about the game itself in this country? What is it that makes you reluctant to go back and be what you are and always will be – a First Division footballer?

GEORGE: It's a mixture, as I've said in the past. I think they do it the wrong way here. They build up their superstars, so-called superstars, and they get them on a pedestal. And the first thing they want to do when they get them there is knock them off again. I don't think they do that in America. I think they do exactly the opposite. If they get someone who's good at their job and brings the crowds in, no matter what he does outside the game or how he performs off the field, they go out of their way to keep him at the top. Because they love their superstars.

MICHAEL: So it's really the price of being a superstar in this country that you object to more than anything else, that you find intolerable?

GEORGE: It's difficult. I don't think they know how to treat their stars. I don't think they've got enough sympathy with them, and it's hard work being a face or a name in England.

MICHAEL: Let's go back now to talk about the pressures that brought about this very sad downfall for you in this game. It's sad to think that you are probably not going to play in English football again. You mentioned the press, and you feel that you've been hard done to by them. First of all, don't you think at times you've played into their hands?

Don't you think that you've courted disaster with your behaviour?

GEORGE: Yeah, when I first started, I was the same as everyone else. I'd love to see my name in the papers and I used to do things to make sure I got my name in the papers. And I still do, because I know at the end of the day that I'm going to benefit from it financially. But you've got to give and take. I originally started it off and maybe courted disaster, but . . . they went overboard, they really did. Some of the things they've said and done . . .

MICHAEL: Like what?

GEORGE: Well, I've forgotten how many times I've taken newspapers to court . . . For instance, one newspaper wrote that I'm a boring little man. Why should anyone be able to write things like that about me? I mean, it doesn't bother me, because I know what they're like, I can take it. But then I think of my parents and people who are involved with me personally who've got to read that. You know newspapers, and they shouldn't be able to get away with it. And they do it because it's me. Let's face it, if I take them to court, it's great for them, they love it, I think.

MICHAEL: What else don't you like? Have there been any attempts to stunt up a story?

GEORGE: Oh, there's been hundreds. I could tell you a hundred stories about things they've done. One newspaper paid a girl fifteen hundred pounds to sleep with me. To get a story.

MICHAEL: Fifteen hundred quid to sleep with you?

GEORGE: Yes. I was annoyed it was only fifteen hundred quid. [AUDIENCE LAUGHTER] No, but things like that, and they do it, seriously.

MICHAEL: What about the start for you, the pressures that you talked about earlier? Not just the press, because I take what you say, that they've treated you badly. On the other hand, I know you well enough to know that you've put your head on the block occasionally. You have courted disaster. But what interests me and a lot of people watching, and a few people in the audience, is that they've got kids for whom football is a big glamorous sport, and they all want to be Georgie Best superstar. Now, you left home when you were fifteen and you were a First Division footballer and an international by the time you were seventeen. When you look back at it now – you've been two years out of the game, you're twenty-nine years old now, you're a more mature man – can you see what went wrong, why you didn't retire at the age of, say, thirty, a millionaire and the biggest name in the world of sport?

GEORGE: I can't really. There were a hell of a lot of things all coming at once. I mean, I had great years from seventeen until I was twenty-five. I had eight great years at Manchester. And I enjoyed it and loved it, and if a kid comes to me now, say at fourteen or fifteen, and wants to become a professional footballer, I'd say certainly. As far as I'm concerned, it's still the greatest sport in the world.

MICHAEL: Yes.

GEORGE: But there's a lot of downfalls. Everyone's individual anyway, so it's going to be difficult, but it's hard for a kid at fifteen to leave home and come into the big world as a professional footballer. And I think it might be an idea if clubs maybe had some person – I don't know what you would call them, public relations, or someone – whose sole purpose is to look after the kids and make sure they have everything they want, someone they could come and see if they had little personal problems.

MICHAEL: Yes.

GEORGE: And it's a tough sport. I mean, some of the kids I've seen, when I first arrived, 98 per cent of them never make it.

MICHAEL: Really, as high as that?

GEORGE: Well, say when I played in 1964 in our youth team. I was looking through the team a couple of weeks ago, and of those that played in the FA Youth Cup final in '64, I think maybe only two made First Division footballers.

MICHAEL: Really?

GEORGE: And for the eight or nine who made it to that team, there were hundreds and hundreds who never quite got into it.

MICHAEL: Yes.

GEORGE: It's a hard game, and that's where it's sad, because a kid comes away at fifteen, and he's away from home for, say, two years. And then at seventeen, the club decides whether to sign him or send him home. That's the real heartbreak. You know, two years of your life, and every kid dreams of being a footballer.

MICHAEL: Yes.

GEORGE: And at seventeen, it's like they're taking your life away. It's sad, the ones that don't make it.

MICHAEL: And of course they're not trained for anything else. That's the point.

GEORGE: I think they are trying to help with that a bit more now than they used to. But, to get back to what you were asking, if I was to say to someone, a kid, 'Yes, certainly become a professional footballer. If you've got the talent and you love it.' But to the parents, 'Just be careful, keep them out of harm. Make sure everything's going all right for them.'

MICHAEL: Would it have been any different for you, do you think, had you been living at home with your parents?

GEORGE: I suppose so. I mean, if I had problems between fifteen and seventeen, I couldn't keep running back to Belfast to ask Mum and Dad what I should do. I had to basically make decisions on my own.

MICHAEL: Yes.

GEORGE: And maybe if there had been someone there . . .
I think it might be an idea for the clubs to have someone
on hand for that sole purpose.

MICHAEL: Yes.

GEORGE: To look after the kids.

MICHAEL: Do you think the clubs have learnt anything from
what happened to you? In other words, if George Best
Mark II went along to Manchester United tomorrow – they
should be so lucky, indeed any club should be so lucky –
do you think the same mistakes might happen?

GEORGE: Possibly, but as I say, I don't know what they can
do about it. I mean, each person is an individual. I probably got myself into more trouble than anybody else, you
know. Through my own fault. But there again, I never felt
there was anyone I could go and discuss it with.

MICHAEL: Yes.

GEORGE: That's why I don't know if they have learnt or if
they ever will learn. I hope so. What I've gone through, I
hope it never happens to anyone else. But I can see it –
over the last few years, it's been happening to other players.

MICHAEL: You think so?

GEORGE: Yes.

MICHAEL: Can I put something to you? One of the most
perceptive critics in British football is Hugh McIlvanney.
And he wrote this about you once: 'I suspect that deep in
his nature, there's a strong self-destructive impulse. Now

and again, he appears to have an irresistible desire to put two fingers up to the whole world.' How true is that?

GEORGE: When I see him, he's in trouble if he wrote that. I don't know, I suppose it's fifty–fifty. I mean, I've done stupid things. It's difficult to say. To be quite honest, all I wanted to do was to be left alone to play football. But I couldn't do it. So I suppose once in a while, if someone was having a go at me, I'd stick two fingers up to them, because I didn't want to take it.

MICHAEL: But let's talk now about the future. Because you're embarking, as you say, on a second career almost now. You're starting again at the age of twenty-nine. What I'm sure people are interested to know is how much you've changed. What's different in George Best, as he's sitting opposite me now, from the one two years ago who'd jacked the game in?

GEORGE: I don't know. I suppose in the two years I've been involved in business more heavily than I have in football. And I'd like to think that personally I've grown up a little bit.

MICHAEL: But let's pick up on three specific areas you've always been criticised for. One is gambling. Have you changed your attitude towards gambling? You used to gamble very heavily, didn't you?

GEORGE: I used to, particularly in the past couple of years. And there again I suppose it was boredom. I had nothing else to do. I didn't know where I was going or what I was doing. It was just something to do, to pass the time, I suppose.

MICHAEL: So, what was the most you ever lost? Or won?

GEORGE: Well, I went to a casino one night and I was losing seventeen thousand pounds. And I couldn't afford that. I couldn't have paid them if I had lost it. But I had a pile of chips. I owed this seventeen thousand. Fortunately, that night things went quite well. I won twenty-six thousand. But when I thought about it afterwards, I thought 'This is crazy. I mean, I'm gambling my life away'. I couldn't afford to gamble. A couple of nights later, I went back again and I think I lost about four or five thousand pounds – and that was it. I'll maybe have a bet on the horses, but I've stopped completely going to casinos.

MICHAEL: What about the booze?

GEORGE: That again. I used to behave in a similar way, I used to go crazy. Again, I don't know whether it was boredom, and needing people's company. I used to just travel from bar to bar and drink. I once sat in a restaurant in London from eleven fifteen in the morning until four o'clock the next morning. Just drinking completely. And having people for company. And crazy things. I mean, I drank a pint of vodka once for a bet – you know, in one go. When I think about it now, it was crazy. It was like Hugh McIlvanney said, I was trying to kill myself. I don't know if that was boredom or nothing to do. And now I have a glass of white wine, a glass of champagne, but nowhere near what I was doing.

MICHAEL: What about women? Have you given them up? [GEORGE LAUGHS] Don't tell me fibs either, Bestie.

GEORGE: You know me too well. Listen, I'm a young, healthy man – why shouldn't I go with women? I mean, there's nothing wrong with it. [AUDIENCE LAUGHTER] It amazes me: I pick newspapers up and they say, 'He goes with women.' What the hell's wrong with that? I enjoy their company and I enjoy being seen with beautiful women, and I don't see there's anything wrong with it. And I'll tell you it doesn't affect my performance on the field. [AUDIENCE LAUGHTER]

MICHAEL: You're not one of those who believes that it weakens you.

GEORGE: I think it's a load of rubbish. I mean, it really is.

MICHAEL: I feel the same, about my performance on television. [AUDIENCE LAUGHTER]

GEORGE: You know, it makes me laugh. I mean, one newspaper came to Spain when I was there. And they threaten you, they say if you don't let us take photographs when you're with women, we'll take them anyway. And then when I pose with the women, I pick up the newspaper a couple of weeks later and they're crucifying me for having my photograph taken with women. The same newspapers. And they had said, 'If you don't let us take the photographs, we'll follow you until we get one, because sooner or later you're going to be seen with a woman and we will take a photograph anyway.'

MICHAEL: Yes.

GEORGE: And then they crucify me for going out with girls.

MICHAEL: Do you think you'll ever have a lasting relationship with a woman? A permanent one?

GEORGE: I'd like to. That might have made a difference as well, if I'd got married and settled down, with maybe a wife and a few kids. But there's never been anyone I've felt like settling down with for the rest of my life. I'd love to,

Home Sweet Home – dream house becomes a prison.

because I love kids. But it hasn't happened. It doesn't bother me. I know sooner or later it will happen.

MICHAEL: The other extraordinary thing is that you've been talking about the massive amount of money which no doubt will come your way. You've never been short of a bob or two, you've always earned a good living since you were seventeen, but you still live in digs with Mrs Fullaway. Park the Maserati outside a council house. It seems incredible. Why's that?

GEORGE: Well, I tried to build a home for myself. I had a house built and I moved in there. And it was like living in a zoo. A goldfish bowl. It was amazing. You know, I had day-trippers coming up, coachloads parking outside my house. They'd arrive with their flasks, tea and sandwiches, and park outside my front door. I was afraid to answer the telephone. I wouldn't answer the door. I used to actually hide in my own house. When the doorbell went, I used to look from behind the curtain before I went to the door. I put an answering machine in and I used to play the machine back to see who was on the phone. It got like that.

MICHAEL: Do people steal things from you as well, from the house?

GEORGE: Oh, they're amazing. I got a phone call from a headmaster at a local school once. Phoned me up, and he said, 'I've had a couple of young kids come into school this morning,' and they were going around school, swapping my goldfish from my pond. You know it was like a swap shop. They were getting six *Dandys* and *Beanos* for a goldfish from my pond. And he wasn't bothered that they were doing it. He just wanted to check that they were my goldfish. [AUDIENCE LAUGHTER] In case they were telling lies.

I ended up asking a pal of mine on the police force near where I used to live – I used to have to phone him to say that I'm going out for dinner at seven thirty. Because people and the press used to park outside the house and would try and follow me in their cars. He used to come round in the police car. And I had an automatic garage. So I used to press a button and drive out, then he used to drive behind me at thirty miles an hour, and I used to shoot off at seventy miles an hour, so that the cars that were following me, if they overtook him, they could be booked for speeding. [AUDIENCE LAUGHTER] All so I could get away and have a fun night.

MICHAEL: Well, now you're embarking on a new career. And no doubt lots of this is going to happen to you again. Do you feel that you are going to be able to cope with it in the future? You're not going to have any more crack-ups like we did before?

GEORGE: Yeah, where I am now, I sort of laugh it off. I treat it as a big joke. I tend to take the mickey out of them. I find it keeps me sane. I mean, they phone up and I give them the most ridiculous stories. Some of the stuff I tell them . . . They print it and it's a load of rubbish. I just make something up because they want a story. So I just give it to them. I mean, they're not going to write nice things, because that won't sell papers.

MICHAEL: Well, I think it's very sad that you're going to go and play football in America. And that seems likely. I really do think it's sad that you're not going to play over here. No hope that sometime in the future you might play English First Division football again?

GEORGE: I shouldn't think so. I mean, the American season is, I think, from April through until August. It's nice because I'm a free agent, and I still like to play in this country. I play games all over the place at the moment. And if the people are still coming to watch me, I'd like to come back and play some games.

MICHAEL: Yes.

GEORGE: But I wouldn't want to throw myself into the rigmarole again. I think the States, it's like a new stage for me. That's the way I look at it. I'm an entertainer, and I've got the whole of America to entertain. And if I can do it, I know they'll come.

MICHAEL: I'm sure you can do it and I wish you all the best, George. George Best, thank you very much indeed. Thank you.

*

It would be eight years before I interviewed him again and it was at a low point in his life. The American Dream had gone sour, as well as his marriage to former model and fitness guru Angie, a marriage that had produced one son, Calum, who he was now also estranged from. His drinking had spiralled out of control to such an extent that he was at last having treatment for alcoholism.

At that time I was spending half the year doing my chat show for Channel 10 in Sydney. As I always did, I offered George a bolthole. He came over to play a few games for the Brisbane Lions, but in reality it was another chance to run for cover. Again, he hadn't moved on. He was still walking round that same circle of Hell, repeating the same reason for his behaviour over and over again like a mantra.

Edited excerpt from interview with George Best
*(*Parkinson *in Australia, 1983)*

MICHAEL: Tracing that back, do you think it was in these early years, when you say you were part of the pop thing, that the seeds of this kind of tragedy were sown?

GEORGE: I suppose so. You know, in those days all I ever thought about was football. It came first, first and foremost.

And to this day, it's still a big love to me. I enjoy it tremendously, and I get a big thrill out of it. I can still feel that buzz from people when I run onto the field. I know I can do things that are still a little bit special, and a little bit different from other people. That excites me, and it's frightening to think one day it's going to be gone. In the early days, playing with that great, great side, it was even more so, because we went out there and nine times out of ten we won.

MICHAEL: Yes.

GEORGE: Then it started to go the other way. You know, seven times out of ten we started to lose. And I wasn't used to it. I was used to being number one. I found that very difficult, to accept there was such a thing as number two. It was something I had to work on. I played for a great team, and I saw them slide a little bit and . . . I took the easy way out. I didn't want to play for them the way it was, but I didn't want to play for another team, so I took the third option. I just opted out for a while and disappeared.

MICHAEL: Well, you had this problem of drinking. Now, I've known you for many, many years. I've known you since you were sixteen, and we've been friends all that time. I never, ever, thought you were an alcoholic. I thought you were a very heavy drinker at times, a social drinker, but not an alcoholic. Yet you say you are.

Drinks all round – George joins Rodney Marsh, Kenny Lynch, Frank Lampard, Alan Ball and Malcolm McDonald at the opening of Bobby Moore's pub in 1976.

GEORGE: Yes, I think you hide it from friends. What was happening was if you and I would go out for a drink and have a nice evening, you'd go home to the wife and kids, but I'd go on to a drinking spot. When I'd finished there, I'd find a spot that opened at nine o'clock in the morning. I never got to the stage where I woke up in the morning looking for a drink, but I became what we call a bad drinker. I think the longest I went was twenty-two days, drinking solidly. Without food. That's when I figured it was a problem. [AUDIENCE LAUGHTER] And actually, it's not a problem, I'm an alcoholic.

I know, because you're a good friend, my closest friends find it more difficult to understand than strangers.

MICHAEL: When you had the twenty-two-day bout, George, can you remember anything about it?

GEORGE: I went through a spell where I couldn't remember anything. I could remember the early part, and maybe the final part. But maybe a week in between where I had a total blackout. And just recently . . . You know, I suppose I'm lucky, because just recently, I met one of the biggest pop stars in the world. He came to see me because he'd gone through the same thing. He told me he'd gone from 1979 to 1980 and lost a complete year of his life through alcohol. Couldn't remember a thing.

MICHAEL: It's terrifying, isn't it?

GEORGE: Yes. Frightening, yes.

MICHAEL: You went for treatment in America, I think I'm right in saying. Twice you went there.

GEORGE: I did, and then again it was frightening. But I was proud of myself, because I was six thousand miles from home, I didn't really know anybody or have any close friends there, and I decided I had to do something about it. And I went in. I was virtually locked up for thirty days, each time, with . . . normal everyday people. There were lawyers there, doctors, a Hell's Angel.

MICHAEL: It's got nothing to do with intelligence, has it, drinking?

GEORGE: No, that's the funny thing. People think of alcoholics or drunks or whatever you want to call them as an old wino lying in the street. It's not true. The highest percentage of people who suffer from alcoholism are very, very intelligent. Including me, of course. [AUDIENCE LAUGHTER]

MICHAEL: Was it a kind of shock therapy, in the place that you went to?

GEORGE: It was. There was a lot of group therapy and then a lot of paperwork. A lot of really looking at yourself. Standing up and looking at yourself in the mirror and saying, 'You're a complete disaster.' The frightening thing from the people in the hospital I went to, they said I hadn't hit rock bottom. I'd come as close as I could. But they were frightened, because I usually did it when things were going well for me.

MICHAEL: Yes, I'd noticed that.

GEORGE: Mmm, as opposed to most of the people in there, who had lost homes, families, kids – you know, everything, money. And had nothing left. It was the final solution. I was usually in there when things were going tremendously well for me. So they couldn't quite figure me out. [AUDIENCE LAUGHTER]

MICHAEL: But, what about now? I notice you talk in the present tense. You say, I *am* an alcoholic. That's part of the therapy, isn't it?

GEORGE: It is.

MICHAEL: You must understand the problem. What are the chances now that you'd go on a bender?

GEORGE: It's a day-to-day thing. It really is, you know. If I pick up a glass of wine and drink it . . . I mean, I love a nice cold glass of wine or champagne with dinner. It's tremendous. But I just have to realise that my system reacts differently to normal people, and if I have that one glass, it's . . . I can't have one glass, I have to continue. It might be two days, it might be three, it might be another twenty-two-day thing. And I don't want to go through that. I have to go to bed every night and slap myself on the back and say, 'Well done.'

MICHAEL: How much do you have to rely on people around you as well? To look after you? Do they see the warning signs coming?

GEORGE: Yes. People close to me do, yes. I didn't think they did. I thought I could hide it. But close friends do see it. And I really don't know when it's going to happen, that's the frightening thing.

MICHAEL: You must have the constitution of a horse, though. Because you've been playing professional football at the top level for, what, twenty years?

GEORGE: Yes. It's coming up to twenty-one years, yes.

MICHAEL: And all the time you were drinking you were playing football, weren't you?

GEORGE: Yes. I think if I hadn't been so fit and trained

regularly – and I still enjoy training, I love training – I'd probably be dead by now. The fact that I was so fit, I got away with a lot. And my ex-wife hates me – she says I should look like ninety-seven instead of thirty-seven. [AUDIENCE LAUGHTER]

MICHAEL: Did you ever, in those low moments, those very low moments of your life, did you ever think of pushing it to the ultimate and committing suicide?

GEORGE: I never got that far . . . I'm too selfish. [AUDIENCE LAUGHTER] At the back of my mind, I used to remember all the good times. Because it wasn't all bad, you know. I've had some tremendous times, I've had a great life. I've been very, very fortunate. I've made a lot of good friends, I've had some good laughs. I still have good laughs. I have to learn that I was wrong to think that I couldn't laugh without a drink. And it's such a load of rubbish, you know. I used to think I couldn't come on and talk to you without having six or seven drinks backstage. Or do anything without a drink – except football, of course.

MICHAEL: Yes. When you look back on your life, the two things you are renowned for, apart from the football, are the drinking, of course, and then the ladies. I mean, you've had one or two in your life. [AUDIENCE LAUGHTER]

GEORGE: What do you mean, 'had one or two'?

MICHAEL: Well, in the biblical sense you've had them. But have you ever kept a count of how many ladies you've known?

GEORGE: No, I wouldn't. I wouldn't insult the ladies by keeping count. It's two thousand, four hundred and seventy-two! [AUDIENCE LAUGHTER] No, I haven't, actually. I've been very fortunate. As I say, it was the pop-star thing and, and the image. I suppose they were always available. And I really was very shy, you know, when I first left home. And I don't know why I did it really. Because you know what I'm like in company: I prefer to sit in the corner, and for some reason . . .

MICHAEL: You don't dance.

GEORGE: I don't dance, I hate dancing.

MICHAEL: That's right.

GEORGE: And I don't like to talk a lot really . . . when I'm drinking. And I'm used to waking up in the mornings with twenty phone numbers, and goodness knows how I got them! [AUDIENCE LAUGHTER] I've been fortunate, I suppose, in that area. For some reason, the British press think there's something wrong with having lots of girlfriends and I . . . don't see anything wrong with it.

The next few years of his life were the stuff of tabloid editors' dreams: bankruptcy, drunken chat-show appearances, a three-month jail sentence for drink-driving and assaulting a police officer. For the generation that had never seen him play, it was impossible to equate this dishevelled man lurching from one crisis to another with the one that had their fathers and grandfathers moist-eyed with sadness and remembrance.

He managed to return his life to a semblance of order in the 1990s with the help of some good people who genuinely liked and cared for him. People like his agent and friend Phil Hughes, his lifelong friend and mine Malcolm Wagner, and his long-term girlfriend Mary Shatila. He, like always, moved on from Mary and got married again, to Alex Pursey, but this time it seemed to work, and through his regular punditry on television and in newspapers he began to repair his reputation and remind people of what an astute thinker about the game he was. But in the background, the boozing and bingeing continued, the lessons remained unlearned, new promises were made and broken, and as he grew older the damage was becoming irreversible.

By the time of our final interview, in 2001, he had been diagnosed with severe liver damage. His liver was operating at less than 20 per cent and he had been put on a waiting list for a transplant. He came on to talk about his latest autobiography, called *Blessed*, which remains, in my opinion, the most honest of the books about him. It's amazing what a near-death experience can do for you.

What was also interesting about this interview was that George was on with David Beckham, then more known for his prowess on the football field than for posing in his pants whilst building Brand Beckham.

There sat two men, the peak of their careers separated by no more than thirty years, united by a gift for football and a level of fame way above that of their fellow footballers. But in one chair sat a young man holding hands with his pop-star wife at his side, certain of his future, secure in himself, whilst in the other sat a diminished figure, looking older than his fifty-five years and still struggling to come to terms with himself and finding a way to live. It was like a tableau from a morality play.

Of all the interviews, this was the closest I ever got to George being honest about himself. It was the one that got closest to his inner thoughts. Afterwards, I felt genuinely hopeful that if he got through this period he could at last free himself of the hidden demons that he tried to drown in liquor. Knowing what happened a few years afterwards, it is now particularly difficult to read of his optimism for the future. Maybe I was stupid to believe him after all the false dawns I had witnessed. But Bestie was like that. Whether on the pitch or in real life, you couldn't help but be beguiled by him.

Edited excerpt from interview with George Best
*(*Parkinson, *2001)*

MICHAEL: What's the latest medical bulletin?

GEORGE: I'm still on a lot of medication, and Alex and I decided to take the drastic step of having the Antabuse put in.

MICHAEL: Antabuse is . . .

GEORGE: A tablet that I tried many years ago, but obviously the way my medical people have looked into alcohol, which they now regard as a disease I suffer from, it's now in there permanently, so even if I wanted to have a drink, I couldn't. It's a very dangerous thing to have in your system, but it's working for me, so far, and hopefully it will continue for a long time. It was a bit frightening what I went through, and I certainly don't want to go through it again, that's for sure.

MICHAEL: No, no. What decided you to actually go into hospital? Because in the past you've always resisted all temptation, George.

GEORGE: I think what it is, Michael, we kid ourselves sometimes. You think, 'Right, OK, I'll stop drinking for three months, or six months, or a year'. But at the end of it, the good old liver recovers and I can go and have a drink. But it's not the way it is. And I got seriously ill. It was Alex who called the medical people. I was actually on my floor, in

Chelsea, where we were living at the time. And I couldn't move. She called the ambulance and they had to pick me up and carry me into hospital. They took me to Chelsea and Westminster and they gave me a jab that made me feel like I was on drugs or something. I recovered very quickly and went home that night. But obviously it wasn't right, I was very seriously ill, and I decided I was very lucky again in a way. I went to see a Professor Williams, who's spent his life researching into the liver. And I do a lot of work with him now, raising money. And it's just . . . I went through a spell where I thought I couldn't be bothered any more.

MICHAEL: You were going to top yourself?

GEORGE: Yes. I thought it would be easier. You know. I had nothing to live for. I didn't think I had.

MICHAEL: Did you plan it?

GEORGE: Yes, yes.

MICHAEL: What were you going to do?

GEORGE: I was going to go and get a bottle of Louis XIII brandy. I was going to get a nice bottle of Dom Pérignon, and take a few pills and get a hammock in Jamaica or the Bahamas somewhere, and that was going to be it. But, funnily enough, in a way, the fact that I almost died sort of changed me, my whole look on life.

MICHAEL: The book you've written, you've called *Blessed*. Well, a lot of people would think, given the last twenty-seven years of your life, that you'd been far from blessed.

GEORGE: I believe that a *lot of* people are born with gifts. I was. And I think you have to work at it, but you've also got to be very lucky in life at times. To be born with something. And I was born with something. I really, really didn't have to work too hard. I did, because I enjoyed training, contrary to what people used to think, and I used to love being fit.

MICHAEL: What's interesting in your book, and we've known each other for a lifetime, is that for the first time you've confronted yourself.

GEORGE: Yes, yes.

MICHAEL: You're a strange lad. I mean, you've always backed off facing up, haven't you . . . in a sense, run away from things?

GEORGE: I have, I've tended to hide in corners . . . whether I didn't want to face reality or I just couldn't be bothered facing it. And my poor old mother couldn't handle it. My dad's as strong – you know my dad – he's as strong as an ox, and he's got a strong character. But my mum couldn't handle it. And it ended up costing her her life in the end.

MICHAEL: She became an alcoholic.

GEORGE: Yes, and . . . for a long time I found it difficult to talk about. It's still difficult to talk about.

MICHAEL: I'm sure it is.

GEORGE: But, you know, it's something you have to. And for a long time, I blamed myself. I thought it was me. But

I now realise, whatever I'd have done, it might have not changed things one way or the other. It might have been a little bit easier for her. But I'd been away from Mum's since I was fifteen. And I certainly couldn't look after her, because I was having enough problems looking after myself. And failing most of the time.

MICHAEL: Do you feel better for having put it down?

GEORGE: Yes. I do, I do.

MICHAEL: There was a time when it was affecting you. You write in the book that when you were twenty-two you started having blackouts, didn't you?

In happier times – celebrating his parents' silver wedding in 1970.

GEORGE: Yes. I mean, we all laugh and talk about it: 'Can't remember where you parked your car the night before.' It seems funny at the time. When you can't remember days and weeks, it's slightly different. And you're drinking fourteen pints of vodka a day – it doesn't help. There wasn't one point, no. It was gradually getting worse, obviously, because at the end of the day, it almost finished me off. But I think the worst period was when I was in America and I was so far away from home. It sounded quite exciting, because it was a new league, and all the best players in the world were there, bringing in big crowds, it was quite exciting. I was living down on the beach in Los Angeles. I had a very successful business. And on the face of it, it seemed perfect, but I was so bored, you know. I was becoming a beach bum. I always had plenty of money and the sunshine and everything else. And, of course, Calum was born. But for some strange reason even that didn't pull me out of it at the time.

MICHAEL: In the book – and I want you to tell this story – you confront the moment that you were at your lowest point. Which was in America, wasn't it?

GEORGE: Yes.

MICHAEL: When you went to the bar with a girl. Tell us what happened.

GEORGE: Well . . . in this country it was easy. I could walk in a bar, like most people who are well known, and someone will send you a drink over. You just sit there for five minutes, someone will buy you a drink eventually. You don't need money here. But in America it was slightly different and . . . I was desperate for a drink one night and I stole from a girl's purse at the bar while she went to the ladies'. Then I knew it was something a little bit serious. Because I've never been a dishonest person, or I hope I haven't in my life. I made up for it, I . . .

MICHAEL: You went back, didn't you?

GEORGE: I went back.

MICHAEL: And gave it to her?

GEORGE: And gave it back to her. But the fact that I'd done it in the first place – I thought, 'What am I doing here?' You know, stealing, for some stupid craving that was killing me.

MICHAEL: Ten bucks.

GEORGE: Yes.

MICHAEL: But that didn't stop you, you see. And the other thing that you went through, it seems to me you did it for other people, not for yourself: you went to Alcoholics Anonymous. You couldn't face it there, could you? You never got on with that.

GEORGE: No. I tried everything. I went . . . I mean, it's a little bit difficult for me to go to Alcoholics *Anonymous*. [AUDIENCE LAUGHTER] You've got a counsellor sending you drinks to your room, it's a bit difficult. Yes, I did, I made efforts, I tried everything. And, you know, it works for a lot of people. A hell of a lot of people go to AA and it saves their lives. But it didn't work for me. I tried private counselling. But I tended to do what I used to do with dear old Sir Matt. I used to sit there and just nod and agree with everything, thinking, 'I can't wait to get out of here, so I can go and have a drink.' But, yes, I made efforts, and I was hospitalised twice in America. I had a lot of help from a lot of people . . . I remember once in the hospital in America, it was an Irish guy who had become a counsellor and had been dry for twenty-odd years. And he said to me, 'You know, we all need a crutch but you've got to realise that one day it might not be there.'

MICHAEL: Yes.

GEORGE: And he said, 'The way I looked at it was like you've got a choice. Switching the light off or on.'

MICHAEL: Yes.

GEORGE: He said, 'It sounds over-simplified, but that's it.'

MICHAEL: Yes.

GEORGE: And one day he said, 'You've got to decide whether you want the light to keep shining, or do you want to switch it off?'

MICHAEL: Thank God you did.

GEORGE: And luckily I've made what I think is the right decision and at the moment life is just great. I mean, compared to what it was just a year ago, it is amazing.

MICHAEL: I suppose you do now live it day to day, don't you?

GEORGE: I have to. I have to. I get up every morning and slap myself on the back and say, 'Well done.'

MICHAEL: But you'd love to play in the era now, wouldn't you? I mean, think of the money, think of all the things. They don't tackle like they used to.

GEORGE: Well, they're not allowed to tackle. I don't think people like Norman Hunter and Billy Bremner and Nobby Stiles would last a game, would they? It would certainly be a little bit easier, yes, but things change. People ask me if I regret that I'm not making the sort of money the players do now. Good luck to them. It's a short life, and you never know from one day to the next. I still pay and go and watch them play, and I enjoy covering the Premiership. I think the Premiership has been absolutely amazing since it started.

MICHAEL: But it's interesting to see, you're thirty years apart, here you sit, and you were the first soccer superstar, front page, back page, you were there, same as David today. And yet the difference is that nowadays there's an industry surrounding David, there's protection. I remember you being totally, absolutely. in a sense, naked, because nobody knew what was happening to you until it was too late. Your agent, I remember, used to live in Huddersfield.

GEORGE: It was a bit weird, you know. Dear old agent, who had just come into the game, and he was stuck in a little office in a square in Huddersfield getting ten thousand letters a week from all these girls sending him knickers. [AUDIENCE LAUGHTER] It aged him very quickly. [AUDIENCE LAUGHTER] Yeah, there's obviously a lot of protection now. Hopefully, people have learned that you have to look after your superstars.

MICHAEL: He's an example, isn't he?

GEORGE: You need good back-up, and I have it today. A little bit too late from a football point of view, but not from my life point of view. And earning a living . . . As you said, I live every day at a time. I'm still not 100 per cent. I'm still on loads of pills. I rattle, my assistant says.

Ken Stanley, back right, watches over clients Alan Ball, Denis Law and George at a launch for their Christmas annuals in 1970.

She's like a nurse now. I can't even say the names of the pills that she's giving me, I don't know what she's giving me, but it's working in one way.

MICHAEL: The other question I've always wanted to ask. You had a reputation with the ladies, I mean second to none. Now, what was the nearest to kick-off that you made love to a woman?

GEORGE: I think it was half-time actually. [APPLAUSE] No, there was this story, a very famous story, when Wilf McGuinness was in charge, and I saw Wilf on Tuesday night and he reminded me that he actually caught me in a lady's room just before we left for a cup semi-final. But he only caught me in a room, he didn't actually . . .

MICHAEL: Oh, he didn't?

GEORGE: No.

MICHAEL: No.

GEORGE: I wouldn't dream of doing something like that before a game.

MICHAEL: No.

GEORGE: The problem was, as he was leaving, he said, 'You'd better play well today,' and the first time I got the ball I fell flat on my face.

Sadly, as we now know, George decided to turn the light off. Frankly, I think he had been in the dark for most of his life. After his passing, the question asked by everyone who ever cared about him, who had ever seen him play, who had ever come across him in their lives, was how did he end up turning his back on the game in his prime and dying at fifty-nine? The one person not interested in the answer to that question was George.

Perhaps the fact is we're asking that question more for ourselves than for George's sake. It was too late for him even when he was alive, but it is the fate of people like him who seemingly walk on air that people like us with our feet on the ground can't help but look up and wonder how and why they fell.

Chapter 7

'NOBODY KNOWS ME'

'They'll forget all the rubbish when I've gone and they'll remember the football. If only one person thinks I'm the best player in the world, that's good enough for me.'

George Best

GEORGE Best received what amounted to a state funeral at Stormont Castle in Belfast on 3 December 2005. It was estimated that nearly 100,000 people lined the route of the funeral procession and a further 25,000 crammed themselves into the Stormont Estate. Former friends and team-mates like Denis Law, Sir Bobby and Paddy Crerand rubbed shoulders with luminaries of world football, politics and celebrity, as well as former team-mates from the Cregagh Boys Club where George had first announced his talent to the world. He was buried next to his mother, Ann, also taken early by that merciless addiction. United again in an embrace with a woman who had loved him unconditionally and whose death in the late 1970s deeply upset and unsettled Best.

When you look back at the images of the day, it is striking to see how many of the faces were captured in a rictus not only of grief but also of shock. It was for all of us difficult to really believe he had gone. Those who were lucky enough to have seen him play, who had watched him time and time again escape the clutches of menacing defenders closing in for the kill, couldn't believe that he hadn't at the last moment nutmegged that dastardly hardman and then turned to us watching fearfully from the sidelines and winked. For those who knew him well, like myself, it was also mixed with a pang of guilt. Could we have done more? Were too many of us content to hang on to his coat-tails, basking in his reflected glory, feeding off the scraps from his table, whilst he, by inches, destroyed himself? Were we too soft on him, unable to separate our hero-worship from real friendship? Did we wait too long before we tried to tell him what he had become? The answer to that question is a qualified yes.

Yes, all of us who were close to him could and should have done more. Our friend was destroying himself in front of our eyes. But when things began to go wrong for George, we were young, living through the most exciting period in our lives, in the company of the most thrilling human being we were ever likely to meet. By the time the dust had settled and we emerged at the end of that mad decade, blinking in disbelief at what had happened but ready to move on to the next stage of our lives and careers, George was already lost to us. I don't believe any of us had the strength or influence to make George change. I don't think any of us really knew what made George tick. I don't think any of us got that close to him. We couldn't: he didn't want us to. George had spent his life evading being tackled, making impossible escapes. He was never going to be pinned down by anyone, defender or concerned friend alike. It was his ball, his life and he was going to keep it to himself.

The truth is, I don't know why he chose to drink himself into oblivion. The pressures that he identified in his interviews were real and made things difficult for him. He was a very shy fifteen-year-old mummy's boy when he first came to Manchester, so homesick that he ran back to Belfast at the first opportunity. It is true that the structures were not in place to look after a vulnerable boy like him, to develop his personality and prepare him for what was to come and what might happen if he didn't make it. That definitely caused him distress in his early days and left him emotionally immature and ill prepared for his future career.

It is also true that because of Munich, Best's importance

GEORGE BEST: A MEMOIR

to Busby's dream became crucial. At seventeen he was placed in the bearpit and at nineteen he had destroyed the might of Lisbon and become the fulcrum of his side: the player Sir Matt pinned all his hopes on. That was a big expectation and responsibility to place on someone who was still basically a child emotionally. Couple this with what happened to Best outside football and the fame his exploits attracted. He came home from Lisbon and found 5,000 letters piled up in his bedroom at the digs he shared with his landlady, Mrs Fullaway. There was no one to tell him how to deal with this, no structure in place to shield him from such excess, to manage expectations, to deal with the flood of offers, commercial and romantic, that came to him daily.

The only support he got was from a decent, capable man called Ken Stanley, who agreed to manage him. This ex-table-tennis champ was an astute businessman and he saw the potential of what George could become commercially. But he was working out of a small office in Huddersfield, trying to learn the art of sports management and marketing whilst it was still in its infancy. George was exposed, unprotected, a lamb to the slaughter. His life became a soap opera and Manchester, once his playground, quickly became a prison.

It is also true that George was deeply frustrated and disillusioned by the way that Manchester United went into decline after the high-water mark of 1968. For someone who was competitive to the point of obsessive, losing at anything was not an option. It was the one thing he repeatedly talked of as the catalyst for his self-destructive and difficult-to-excuse behaviour in the later years of his Manchester United career. He was once interviewed by that doyen of sports journalism, and a man I am proud to call a friend, Hugh McIlvanney, who asked the same question as I had done on numerous occasions: Why?

'It had nothing to do with women and booze, car crashes or court cases. It was purely and simply football. Losing wasn't in my vocabulary. I had been conditioned from boyhood to win, to go out and dominate the opposition. When the wonderful players I had been brought up with – Charlton, Law, Crerand, Stiles – went into decline, United made no real attempt to buy the best replacements available. I was left struggling among fellas who should not have been allowed through the door at Old Trafford. I was doing it on my own and I was just a kid. It sickened me to the heart that we ended up being just about the worst team in the First Division and went on to drop into the Second.'

It would therefore be easy to lay much of the blame for

the problems that George suffered at the door of Manchester United and in particular Sir Matt Busby. But it is an unfair accusation and fundamentally untrue. There had never been a footballer like George. There had been no obvious build-up to him. He was radically different from anything and anyone that had come before. Football clubs and Sir Matt were still managing the players and the club with the rules and attitudes of the 1950s. It was like parents living in the pre-computer age trying to bring up a child who turns up one day with a smartphone and an Instagram account. It wasn't a clash of cultures, because there was such a gulf between how they thought George should behave and what George's life was really like that they might as well have been not merely on different planets but in different universes.

Their tried-and-tested methods for looking after players were as effective on George as firing a pea at a juggernaut. Placing a boy in digs with a solid landlady was a traditional and time-honoured way of ensuring a safe extension of the family home and a place where the expected standards of behaviour could be inculcated. But what if that family home becomes a magnet for every girl in town, and the boy who lives there suddenly becomes so rich that he can go out all night, every night, and buy an E-type Jag, which he parks outside.

The usual solution, if a player outgrew the digs and became a regular first-teamer, was for Sir Matt to suggest that he should get married, buy a nice house in the suburbs and settle down in domestic bliss. Indeed, he did suggest this on several occasions during his regular dressing-down sessions, when George would count the animals on the wallpaper behind Sir Matt's head. George did get engaged during the 1960s, I think only to shock Busby, but he was never serious and saw no reason to clip his wings when he could have the pick of any girl he desired. He did buy a house, and although the ill-advised choice of design turned it into a real-life 'goldfish bowl', no one could really have imagined that his domestic idyll would turn into a no-go zone for him, transformed into a human zoo, with George as the main attraction.

As a last resort, when Frank O'Farrell was manager, they persuaded him to lodge with his team-mate and best friend, Paddy Crerand, in the hope that Paddy's solid domestic life would act as an inspiration and a calming influence. It was an unmitigated disaster. The lodger was often absent. The landlord and landlady became an answering service for a string of lovesick and predatory women. It was such a farce that I lampooned this period in my column for the *Sunday Times*. Under the title 'Mrs Crerand's Diary'

The reluctant landlady and landlord – Noreen and Paddy Crerand.

I imagined what life was like with the most famous footballer in the world as your lodger. Here's a taste:

Monday

Our new lodger arrived today. What a commotion. We've given him upstairs and the lounge downstairs and Paddy and I are living in the kitchen. Still, it's only temporary until he gets married and makes a nest of his own. He's such a lovely-looking boy and very quiet. Ooops, there's the phone again. I'll have to answer it because our lodger has gone to town to have his hair done and Paddy's gone with him to make sure he doesn't get knocked down crossing Deansgate. Be back in a minute . . .

Well I never, it was some girl from Finland or one of those places, who said she'd come over specially to give our lodger a personal massage. I told her we could do without that sort of thing in Chorlton-cum-Hardy. Ah well, I've no more time for tittle-tattle. I've got to make the dinner. Steak and chips and mushy peas. As Paddy's always telling me, you've got to put back what you sweat away.

Tuesday

That nice Mr O'Farrell paid a call today just to see if our lodger was settling in nicely. I asked him if it was all right to give him a key to the front door, but Mr O'Farrell said he thought not just yet. Perhaps in a year or two when he's nearing thirty, he said. Then he'll be able to come and go as he pleases. Of course, he might get married before that.

He's certainly very popular with the girls. The phone never stops ringing and it's always for our lodger. He doesn't bother though. What with training and having his hair done he doesn't get much time nowadays.

Ah well, enough of this tittle-tattle. Time to go upstairs and run his bath and then time for dinner. Tonight it's his favourite – sausage, egg and chips and rice pudding. As Paddy's always telling me, we've got to build him up.

Wednesday

He's been with us three days now and not a bit of trouble. He's as good as gold. They're out at present. Paddy has taken him for a walk in the park. That girl from Finland was on the phone again today saying if she couldn't massage George could she give my Paddy a rub-down? I told her to ring Maine Road and ask for Malcolm Allison. Saucy cat.

It's so peaceful with them out of the house. When they are at home they are so boisterous and noisy. Our lodger likes the telly and the radiogram switched on at the same time. Also he uses the fretwork set that kind Mr O'Farrell gave him the other day.

'Idle hands make mischief,' said Mr O'Farrell in that nice voice of his. How true. But our lodger has had his hands full ever since and already he's nearly finished making a plywood model of the Skol Hotel, Marbella. He's such a clever little fellow really.

Ah well, enough of this daydreaming. Time to put the chips on. As Mr O'Farrell said the other day: 'The First Division Championship is won or lost in the frying pan.'

Thursday

Sir Matt called today with some flowers for me and a jigsaw for our lodger. He wasn't in because he had gone to town to have his hair done. Sir Matt wasn't cross or anything. He said he was used to George not being where he wanted him to be, if you know what I mean.

A traffic warden came to see me soon after Sir Matt had departed. Wanted to know why our car was parked in the street. When I explained that our garage was full with our lodger's cars she said it was perfectly all right in the circumstances and could she have two signed photographs for her sister's children in Cleethorpes.

For dinner tonight I've bought something special – a packet of frozen paella and a bottle of Spanish wine – because our lodger talks of nothing else but the good times he had when he went for a quiet holiday with sixty of his friends to the Costa del Sol.

He enjoyed the meal and said he particularly liked the chips I made to go with the paella.

Friday

Panic stations! Our lodger got lost today. Paddy was very upset but it wasn't his fault. They went out for a walk and while Paddy was buying some frozen chips in the High Street, our lodger wandered off by himself. Well, we were all so worried until we got this message from the sergeant at Chorlton-cum-Hardy police station that they'd found him outside his old house, which has been converted into a supermarket.

When Mr O'Farrell heard our lodger was missing he was very angry, but later he calmed down and came over personally to deliver a blow-football set which he thought might while away many a happy hour. We didn't play tonight because our lodger wanted to take us out for a meal to say thank you for having him.

He took us to a Chinese restaurant where we had the best steak and chips we've had for ages. As that nice Mr O'Farrell said, a full stomach and a contented mind are what our lodger wants.

*

The problem was that George was living the life of a modern-day footballer when the idea of a 'modern-day footballer' hadn't even been thought of. He was worshipped by women, young and old, who were just learning the rudiments of celebrity-idol worship and, let's face it, in some cases celebrity-stalking. He was at the centre of a whirlwind and every person wanted a piece of him. They wanted to come and look at this alien creature who had arrived overnight to live amongst them, and if they were young, try to live like him, and if they were older, shake their heads in wonder. How on earth could Sir Matt, his fellow players or anyone working at the club itself understand what they were dealing with and intervene in any meaningful way?

Perhaps, if I'm honest, the one way that Sir Matt did let him down was to be too indulgent with him. He left him out of team talks but he also left him out of the need to behave in a way that didn't bring the club into disrepute or make his team-mates think it was one rule for George and one rule for them. The problem was Sir Matt looked at him like a son. A prodigal one maybe, but still a son, and a footballer who made his vision of how the game should be played come true. When he looked at him, he saw the ghost of Duncan Edwards and his eyes misted over and clouded his judgement.

But Sir Matt was also a pragmatist, if he was going to win more cups, more league titles, George was the key, and if keeping him on the pitch meant letting him have more rope than the others, then so be it. George, for his part, was used to this kind of treatment. He had always been indulged. He was the first born, the apple of his mother's eye; his father, Dickie, was a kind and gentle man. George knew how to get what he wanted and he played Busby like a harp.

However, it is undeniably true that the Manchester United team went into a decline after the European Cup and more and more pressure to win games singlehandedly fell on George. They were never a truly great side and they were already past their peak when they won the European Cup. There was a need for fresh blood not only on the field but in the manager's chair, where Sir Matt, having achieved his dream, was exhausted and broken by the effort and was afterwards never the same man or manager again. But the ghosts of Munich still hung heavy over Old Trafford and it seemed like sacrilege to even suggest that the survivors of that fateful day and the players and architect of their European success should be moved on. Instead, they were left to choose their own time of departure, with the result that the team began to rot from the head down. Even when Sir Matt did finally relinquish the manager's role, in 1969, the aftermath was akin to the recent botched succession plan after Sir Alex Ferguson stepped down as manager. Sir Matt stayed around as the general manager, still using his old office, whilst the likes of Wilf McGuinness and Frank O'Farrell, who were appointed to manage the club between 1969 and 1972, tried to rebuild the house that Sir Matt built with one hand tied behind their back and the revered ex-'Gaffer' still stalking the corridors, offering his opinion, a power in the boardroom. Moreover, these managers were not Mourinho or Guardiola, but honest, decent men who were promoted far beyond their experience and abilities to fill the shoes of a giant.

But none of it, in my opinion, really explains what happened to George. He loved the fame and adulation. I know, because I was there. He wouldn't have changed the lifestyle for anything. He wasn't a victim; he was a willing participant, albeit caught up in a whirl of forces he couldn't understand. He was happy to explore every aspect of the brave new world he had partly created and inadvertently found himself at the centre of. He had a whale of a time and, yes, it did turn sour at times, but he never hid himself away. There was a side of him that courted the drama his fame provoked, like the time in 1971 when he holed himself up in his latest girlfriend Sinead Cusack's flat after missing training and, surprise, surprise, the UK's press camped outside her door.

He knew what he was doing when he wore that sombrero on his return from Lisbon in 1966 and he was always ready with a quote or a quip for an intrepid pressman, even when he was 'abroad' and incommunicado. That's not to say that the pressure of this 24/7 curiosity about all aspects of his life wasn't a real burden, but the good outweighed the bad. Yes, the fame did also take on a darker edge, which always happens with people of George's profile, and it certainly contributed to a worsening of his mother's drinking when she began to receive unwelcome and deeply unpleasant observations about her beloved son in person and through her postbox. When she died, George blamed himself, believing the pressure of his fame had hounded her to her death. It was a difficult time for him, but he was on the slide well before that awful event happened.

Yes, Manchester United and the football they were playing frustrated him. He could have left – there were offers from Real Madrid and Inter Milan – but he stayed and behaved in a petulant and self-indulgent manner. Now the senior player as well as the talisman, the club looked to him for leadership. But the moments of genius became rarer, the behaviour on and off the pitch more inexplicable and unacceptable. The fact is, his lifestyle was catching up with him. Too much carousing and not enough training meant he was also in decline alongside his beloved United. The frustration he felt was as much at himself as at the fact his team was losing. He wouldn't admit it, though. It was a theme he would repeat throughout his life. Always somebody else's fault: too much publicity; it's the press's fault; too little success on the football field; it's his team-mates' or the manager's fault; too much excess in his private life; it's because people won't leave him alone. He would never turn his sharp mind upon himself and try and see what it was inside him that made him behave in a way that caused people around him to wince and worry.

Hugh McIlvanney believes that George was lost to us the moment a drink passed his lips. There was a family history of alcoholism and he had inherited a predisposition to the condition. What started as a crutch to allow an incredibly shy and immature boy feel comfortable in a man's world ended up consuming his soul. The real pressures he felt and all that came with being George Best were not the cause. It was a compulsion he could not control.

There is much merit in this view. George undeniably had an addictive, excessive personality that didn't know when to stop. He wanted to win obsessively, he gambled recklessly, drank foolishly, loved uninhibitedly. His whole life was about the next goal, the next win, the next girl, the next drink. If one didn't satisfy him then he tried the other, and so on until it became a never-ending, pointless merry-go-round. But it was the drink that really claimed him.

There is a lot of recent research and evidence to back up Hugh's claim, but alongside this I believe there is something more than just the fact he was suffering from a genetic illness that sprang to life the moment he took a drink. He was an alcoholic. He was one when I was a friend of his in Manchester, but then it is difficult to start pointing a finger at someone when your own drinking is at bacchanalian proportions. I've written in the past about my own struggles with drink. There was a time, following my father's death, when I got so bad that Mary gave me an ultimatum. I, in George's words, decided to keep the light on. It doesn't make me a better person than George, just different. Unlike me, there was something in George that made him not care enough to want to carry on living. Not personal vanity, not a career, not a wife, not a child, not a lover, not friends or even surviving family members mattered enough for him, when given another precious chance of life, to give up the booze.

The real tragedy of George Best's life was that despite what others saw, despite what he had given to others, he saw no point in it. His life effectively stopped when he walked out of Old Trafford aged twenty-seven. From then on he never moved forward, he became stuck in a cycle of behaviour that hadn't changed since the middle Sixties. It was as if he was looking for something he had lost and had to keep doubling back to find it before he could move on. He could find no purpose. George Best, who could command a football field like no other player I have seen before or since, simply didn't know how to live.

It is difficult to place yourself in the shoes of someone like George. People that gifted see the world in a different way from the rest of us. They are ultimately dissatisfied souls because they believe they can achieve perfection in the area in which they reign supreme over the rest of us, but then find it difficult to accept they are still prone to mistakes and lapses like us mere mortals. Moreover, they often find the inability to transfer their mastery on the field of play to the field of everyday life more difficult to accept than the rest of us who stumble happily and unhappily through our lives.

In the end, for people like George, true happiness is hard to find. Particularly given that all that he went through and experienced as a vulnerable, immature young man, he went through basically alone. If George had had the sophisticated support systems that exist for sportsmen today, perhaps his alcoholism would have been seen earlier and dealt with before it really took hold. Maybe more would have been done to prepare him psychologically for the fame and riches that his talent and looks would obviously attract. He wouldn't have been left to freewheel out of control. Perhaps then George could've been saved. Perhaps, in the final analysis, the real tragedy of George Best was that he was born out of time.

I've always wondered what would have happened if George had been in his early twenties now. He would still have been top of the pile, but he wouldn't have felt so different, so separate from the rest of his team-mates and colleagues in the game. What would he have achieved on modern-day pitches, flat as billiard tables? In a game that is nowadays virtually a non-contact sport because of the protection afforded players, Lionel Messi and Cristiano Ronaldo might just have to make do with battling over second and third place in the Ballon d'Or. Imagine Best working with a Guardiola! How much would such a complete player be worth now? What wages could he have commanded? Moreover, how much would Brand Best have earned outside the sport if he was surrounded by a sophisticated PR and management machine that would have protected his image, massaged the headlines and perhaps talked some sense into him when he began tottering off the rails?

The influence of Best on the game of football and the lifestyles of modern-day footballers cannot be overestimated. And that, above all things, is his legacy. George Best is godfather to Beckham, Ronaldo, Messi, Neymar and their ilk. He began the process that transformed football from a game played and watched by men in cloth caps and set it on the road to becoming the world's biggest sporting multinational, supported by blue-chip brands, and the billions of broadcasters making millionaires of even average talent and turning the best into global brands.

George was a good friend to me and my family. Yes, there were aspects of him that I didn't like, times when his behaviour, particularly towards women, crossed the line from what I thought was acceptable, but in the end I couldn't help but like him, couldn't help but care about him and try to help him. He found all this public navel-gazing about the whys and wherefores of his behaviour and life perplexing, as much as he found the theories they came up with uninteresting. I believe him when he says, 'Nobody knows me.' The problem is, I'm not sure he did either. He needed help to guide him through the maelstrom of his early life and none was there.

My friend now has an airport named after him and by the time of the publication of this book a hotel bearing his name will have opened. I do hope they have a George Best Bridal Suite. He would have liked that. The quote at the top of this chapter indicates what he would really like to be remembered for. So, George, if you're listening, I think you were the best player in the world then and now. It's always difficult to compare different eras, different generations, except that I know you could play in this one but I'm not so sure Messi could have played in yours. Rest in Peace, my friend.

Chapter 8

ENDPIECE

George, ready for another family game in the Parkinson back garden.

THIS book has been a family affair. It was my eldest son, Andrew, who planted the seed of the idea that we should follow up the Muhammad Ali book with a similar one about George. My middle son Nick keeps the memory of that glorious time and team alive by regularly hosting the Manchester United old boys. My collaborator on the Ali book was my youngest son, Michael, who has produced me and run my production company for the last fifteen-odd years. He helped me with the writing of the historical background to Muhammad's life and has also co-written this one. It's good having children when you can put them to work – they tend to be cheaper and you can still give them a clip round the ear if they become troublesome without fear of an employment tribunal.

But it is also a family affair in the sense that for many years before I lost touch with George he was part of the family, and each of us has different memories of him. I thought as a conclusion to this book it would be good to get my co-author's thoughts on the man he played football with in our back garden.

George and Me by Michael Parkinson Jnr, aged 50 and a bit

I had a schizophrenic childhood. Not in the sense that I suffered from mental illness, though there are times my father questions this. He blames the Celtic genes from my mother. I blame having to work with him.

No, it was schizophrenic in that I grew up when my father was at the height of his fame. On the one hand, I had an entirely normal upbringing: I went to the local school, I was never given a sense of entitlement or made to feel I was different or special just because I had a famous father. And yet on the other hand, I was once in a restaurant when Charlie Chaplin performed for me and my brothers the famous bread-roll dance from his film *The Gold Rush*. I once sat on Eric Morecambe's knee – and, no, it didn't become an issue in later life. I was babysat by Babs from Pan's People – and yes, men of a certain age, she did tuck me up in bed. And, as has been mentioned, I played football with George Best.

Most people believed me when I told them these things, all except one person. Surprisingly, it was a nun. I went to the local Catholic primary school, where I was taught by nuns, all of whom were sadists clothed as Brides of Christ. But that's for another book. George had been down for the weekend and as usual he arrived laden with gifts: football shirts, bags, boots and, of course, balls. It was 'Hello Mike, hello Mary' and out into the garden for another round of the-Parkinson-brothers-pointlessly-chase-George-around-the-garden-as-he-weaves-this-way-and-that-trying-to-get-a-touch-of-the-ball.

I can testify to George's obsessive desire to keep the ball to himself, because in all the time we played with him I don't think anybody else got a kick. We all had our different strategies. The eldest brother, Andrew, was a languid youth and a decent footballer who modelled himself on his hero Franz Beckenbauer. He would gracefully lope alongside George, looking to take the ball cleanly off his foot in the manner of Bobby Moore tackling Pelé in that famous World Cup match in 1970. The middle brother, Nicholas, was an altogether different prospect. He approached football in much the same way as those hard men of old. Being pursued by Nicholas must have taken George back to the days when 'Chopper Harris' was trying to cut him off at the knees. My own performance can best be described as 'headless chicken', punctuated by bouts of frustrated crying, which were soothed by a visit inside to my mum and a liberal application of chocolate.

It is true that we were joined in this fruitless enterprise by the family cat. He was called Mitchum, after the actor Robert Mitchum, because he was big and handsome. He was also a hunter extraordinaire. Nothing escaped him. When we first moved into the house, the garden was a bucolic paradise, full of gentle birdsong, the rustle of woodland creatures and the quacking of nearby ducks. After Mitchum arrived it became a wasteland, a no-go zone. Even humans were circumspect when they went into our garden. He was the local feline hitman. We used to hire him out, at extortionate rates, to local families with a squirrel problem. So you can see why he fancied getting hold of this moving spherical object. But even this top-of-the-food-chain predator got nowhere near it. In desperation, he decided to change tactics. Rather than rely on his ground-attack skills, a genetic memory from his bigger cousins made him take to the nearby trees, and when the ball came close to where he was waiting he would leap panther-like from the branch towards the ball, only to discover it was, as usual, not there any more – and a spectacular face-plant ensued.

I wish we had been able to film these encounters, because it must have been a sight to behold. A dive-bombing cat. Andrew, erect, almost diffident in approach, waiting for his moment. Nicholas, hunched over, bull-like, his new and ill-advised Kevin Keegan perm stuck by sweat to his forehead, swinging legs and arms like a malfunctioning threshing machine. Myself often facing the wrong way to this group, seemingly playing a different game. And in the middle of this mayhem was George, in his element, a great smile on his face. For my part, I can testify that I witnessed at first hand ball control of such speed and deftness that it almost defied belief.

The following Monday I went to school and the nun asked us what we had done at the weekend. My classmates proffered the usual descriptions of visits to art galleries, museums, the theatre – all lies, of course. When my turn came, like a good Catholic boy, I told the absolute truth and said I had played football with George Best. There was a deafening silence. Like a gunslinger, the nun narrowed her eyes under her wimple and asked me to think carefully, because God hates a liar. I repeated the claim and suddenly my classmates found desperately interesting things to look at on the ceiling, or the floor, or out of the window. I was in for it now. And I was. An hour's detention, with ten Our Fathers and ten Hail Marys, plus a good deal of thinking about my immortal soul.

Goodness knows what punishment would have been visited on me if I had told her about the other thing I did with George Best. Namely, take him a cup of tea whilst he was in bed, only to discover that the nice lady he had brought with him didn't seem to be there any more, though I distinctly heard giggles coming from under the covers. Slightly perplexed, I asked my mum what could have happened to the woman. 'They're probably playing hide-and-seek,' she said. I wonder if my mum then went to have a think about her immortal soul.

Bristling with injustice, I was determined to clear my name. So the next time George came down I told him what had happened with the nun and he asked me to get him a pen. He signed a football with a message which read, 'To Sister X, Michael did play football with me, Lots of Love, George Best.' I took it to school and triumphantly presented it to her. After reading it, I didn't get an apology, but I am sure I saw her blush. I wonder how many Our Fathers and Hail Marys she did that night.

George was a lovely man with a real affinity with children. He undoubtedly felt more comfortable with them. As we became adults, my brothers and I would separately see George occasionally, but that easy intimacy had gone. A friend of mine used to have a flat near the Phene Arms pub in Chelsea, which was a favourite haunt of George's. I would see him there occasionally and of course go over to speak to him. He was always polite, asking after Mum and Dad, but then he would make his excuses and leave the pub. It would be easy for me to come up with some trite theory about why this was the case, but only he will know why he felt so uncomfortable seeing me again.

My generation sadly saw him as the figure portrayed in the tabloids, the Bestie of the myriad articles about boozing and birding. Outlandish and often apocryphal stories about him abounded, usually involving iterations of a Miss World, champagne bottles and cash on a hotel bed. In contrast, proof of his football genius was scarce. I do remember seeing a grainy film of his wonder goal for the

San Jose Earthquakes, when he waltzed through the opposition's outfield players before beating the keeper, and I saw him live in what amounted to little more than exhibition matches for Fulham with Rodney Marsh. But that was not enough to convince me or people of my age that he was the player that our dads said he was.

Without the leavening effect of having seen him play in his prime, my generation could only go on what we saw, and what we saw was becoming increasingly easy to dismiss as a self-obsessed drunk, living on past glories, who blamed the world for all that had befallen him and took no responsibility for any of his actions. Unlike my contemporaries, however, I had met George. I did see, albeit through a child's eyes, what he could do, what he was like, and I saw the effect he had on people often just as famous and successful as him. So for me this book has been a difficult process of trying to bring together two halves of a picture, a picture made up of the man I knew as a child and the man I heard about as an adult via the mass media.

As I began work on the book, toiling at the coalface whilst my father lay Barbara Cartland-like on his chaise longue, dictating bon mots for an hour or so before departing for lunch, it became clear that we needed a shape and narrative that would have a different flavour from the traditional biographical approach. The key for me lay in the previous book we worked on together, *Muhammad Ali: A Memoir*. The more research on George I did, the more I was struck by how much Ali and Best had in common, and not just the fact that they were game-changing, era-defining sporting talents.

The parallels between the two and the shared themes of their life allowed me to indulge a fantasy which gave me a way into this book. I imagined a fictitious meeting between the two, prior to the first television interview in 1971, when Ali took a detour to the Slack Alice nightclub in Deansgate, Manchester, to see what all the fuss was about. I imagine him prowling down the stairs, the only man who could have diverted the attention of every woman in the club away from George. He walks up to Bestie and opens with one of his favourite gambits, 'You're almost as pretty as me,' except this time it would be the truth. Ali would have refused a drink but definitely taken part in George's appreciation of the local talent.

It would have been a perfect time for them to meet. Both were at a crossroads in their respective sporting careers. Muhammad, coming back from his ban for refusing the Vietnam draft, smarting from a loss to Frasier, trying to resurrect his career from the bottom of the heavyweight pile. George, disgruntled and frustrated by carrying a team in terminal decline since the high point of 1968 and struggling to live with a fame that was both unprecedented and claustrophobic. Two men with outrageous gifts, determined to be the best there has ever been. Both seeing their respective arenas as stages on which to torment their opponents and entertain the crowd, and in the process changing the perception and demographic of their sport. Both charismatic and bright, both inadvertently becoming figureheads, one political and one cultural, for the defining movements of their generation. And yet at the time of this imaginary meeting both of their futures are clouded by doubt. In my fantasy they spend the evening together sharing their hopes and dreams, the triumphs and disasters, the pressures of fame and the weight of expectation. At the end they part as friends. Ali, as always, has the last word, 'You're not as dumb as you look,' and George is left with a feeling that perhaps there was a different turning to take at his personal crossroads.

But, sadly, it never happened the way I imagined it. Muhammad, like a modern-day Jason, went on a journey, slaying monsters in pursuit of the Golden Fleece of his lost heavyweight crown. George, on the other hand, like a modern-day Achilles, turned his back on the world and sulked in his ships on the shores of Troy, otherwise known as the Brown Bull pub, Salford. Their lives did conjoin at the end when they both died tragically and prematurely, destroyed in different ways by the sports they graced. The difference is that with Muhammad, we were not left wondering, 'What if?' Interestingly in the course of researching the book I learnt from George's sister Barbara that Ali did in fact meet George one night in Annabel's night club in Mayfair. They were obviously both in training! Oh, to have been a fly on the wall for that meeting.

The point of all this fantastical pondering was to try and fathom why two men with so much in common, so similar in so many ways, decided at a crucial time of their lives to take radically different paths.

My father and the others mentioned in the book knew George much better than me, so I won't insult them or him by suggesting my own theory as to why George turned his back on the world at such a young age. But what I can talk about with some authority is the condition that most young people seem to want to suffer from nowadays, and that's fame. It might look like a great way to get more money, to get invites to trendier parties, to get better-looking partners, to get the life you see in the glossies, but it can be a cruel mistress that distorts and deforms the personality of the person who suffers from it, and I use that word advisedly.

I was lucky. Both my parents were very famous, with my father regularly being watched by 11 million people on a Saturday night, whilst my mother became one of the voices of and definitely the fashion icon for stay-at-home mums when she was on the magazine show *Good Afternoon*. Yet neither had their head turned by it. Well, perhaps occasionally my father's head tweaked a little, but fortunately he did prevent it from doing the full *Exorcist* rotation. I think, looking back, the reason they didn't was because fame came to them relatively late in their lives, when they were already married, had a mortgage and three mewling and puking children. The family home and the family were the bedrock of their lives, and although the premieres and nights out with famous friends were fun, what mattered was what was behind their front door.

Now, I'm not painting my childhood as an episode of *The Waltons*. Let's be honest, people in the public eye who get famous for what they do tend not to be the sort of people who win Parent of the Year. But I'm working with one of them and I still talk to the other, so they couldn't have been that bad. As Dad explained earlier, the occasion he came closest to losing his equilibrium was not caused by a rampant ego and the onset of a God complex but by the death of his beloved father, who he missed terribly.

George was the most famous footballer on the planet before he was mentally and emotionally out of short trousers. His head wasn't simply turned, it was spinning like a toy top. Conquering Roman generals who, as a reward, were allowed a triumphal procession through the streets of Rome had as a companion in their chariot a slave whose job it was to keep the general's feet on the ground by whispering in his ear, 'You are but a man.' All George had whispered in his were sweet and not-so-sweet nothings, offers of a drink and lucrative contracts. It is no wonder he began to behave in a fashion that gave the impression he existed in a different moral universe from the rest of us. Excess is the bedfellow of fame and, as we know, George didn't mind how many people shared his bed. Nowadays a press release from the management citing tiredness or a 'virus', a spell in rehab and retirement from public life for the duration would be the order of the day. George was hauled into Sir Matt's office and told to find himself a nice girl and get married. It would be funny if the consequences weren't so tragic.

Through my early life and my job I have seen from the outside what fame can do to a person when the consequences of it are allowed to be experienced without a check or balance. The result can be even worse if the fame arrives when the person is young. The erratic, unreasonable and destructive behaviour is accompanied by a kind of emotional arrested development. If you don't say no to a child, how will they ever learn right from wrong, and without that basic framework, how will that young person ever hope to learn how to live?

I agree with my dad that there was something deep inside George that prevented him from taking real joy from anything he did. He also had that destructive streak common to the Celts that makes them fascinated to take a peek over the abyss. I remember watching a *Parkinson* interview with Sir Richard Burton where he explained this trait. He said, 'I think we do like precipices. We go towards them and withdraw temporarily. Sometimes we go over the edge . . . I did wake up one morning and realise how splendidly rich and extraordinary the world was, and that I couldn't bear its richness and its beauty, and so . . . I thought it best to leave it.'

But I also believe that, because of the unique set of circumstances that made George an idol before he knew who he was, he never really grew up and his personality became shaped by the unreality of fan worship and idolatry. No wonder he ran away when things soured or he couldn't get his own way; no wonder he blamed others for things he did; no wonder he drank to fill the hole where a fully grown-up person should have been.

I feel sorry for George. I know he would have hated anyone to say that, but I see him as an innocent victim of circumstances at a time when no one had the requisite tools to save him. It was a wasted life, and not because he left football so young. That was his choice and we shouldn't, like petulant children, whine that he cheated us. It was, of course, his life and he was not created to be a performing monkey for our benefit. It wasn't a wasted life because he drank too much and became an alcoholic. He is not alone in that, and when all is said and done it was his body. (One thing about him I do find difficult to excuse, however, is that he chose to drink through a liver that was gifted to him, which was an insult to the donor and their family.) No, it was a wasted life because it seemed to me he lived it as if preserved in aspic. After he left United, he kept on repeating the life he had when he was in the dog days of his Manchester career. For me, George didn't have a life, he had a prison sentence.

I rather admire the fact that George seemed eminently uninterested in trying to discover his hidden depths. I rather admire that generation's stoicism, exemplified by Sir Bobby's refusal to feel sorry for himself after Munich and deciding to play rather than take some time out. I wish we could now just leave George in peace. Of course, it'll never happen, because no one will ever find the answer to the question that this book asks about George, and we are therefore eternally curious about him.

I write this in an office situated in the garden where long ago I played football with George Best. I can even see the tree from which Mitchum the killer cat launched himself. A while ago my parents' gardener found an old football in some thick foliage that he was clearing. I know George wouldn't have put it in there, but I wonder if we did once get the ball off him after all . . .

PHOTOGRAPHIC ACKNOWLEDGEMENTS

The author and publisher would like to thank the following for permission to reproduce photographs:

Bob Thomas/Getty Images, Rolls Press/Popperfoto/Getty Images, Popperfoto/Getty Images, Mirrorpix, Empics/PA Images, Peter Robinson/EMPICS Sport/PA Images, Uwe Kraft / imageBROKER/REX/Shutterstock, Elisa Estrada/ Real Madrid via Getty Images, Yoan Valat / Epa/REX/ Shutterstock, Cathal McNaughton/PA Archive/PA Images, Colorsport/REX/Shutterstock, Fox Photos/Getty Images, S&G/S&G and Barratts/EMPICS Sport/PA Images, Bob Thomas/Popperfoto/Getty Images, PA Archive/PA Images, David Goddard/Getty Images, Bob Thomas/Getty Images, Empics/PA Archive/PA Images, Daily Sketch/Associated

INDEX

devotion to football 50–1,
  53, 128–9
disillusionment with British
  football xviii–xix, 114–15
and the drinking ix, xii, xiv,
  77, 82–90, 96–7, 99–100,
  102, 104, 112, 122–3,
  128–39, 142–5, 147–8,
  153, 155, 167–70, 181–2,
  188–9
    'blackouts' 131, 142
    how it didn't make him
  happy xii
    liver damage 136,
  139
    liver transplant 189
    never wanting to stop x
and the fame x–xi, xxii, 44,
  60–4, 67–8, 71–2, 77, 82,
  110–11, 115–17, 128,
  145–7, 154, 156, 163,
  165–6, 170, 183–4,
  185–9
    fan mail x, 68, 146,
  154
    as 'Fifth Beatle' 60, 64
    first pop star of football
  xiv, 128
    lack of protection ix,
  145–6, 153–4, 170–1,
  188–9
    sex symbol 62, 64

fiftieth anniversary of being
  crowned European Player
  of the Year xix
fiftieth birthday x
fights 88, 89–90,
  109–10
football career after
  Manchester United 81–2,
  112–14, 121, 127, 142,
  181–2
football skills
    Alex Ferguson on 50
    ball control 41
    Bobby Charlton on
  53–5
    calmness before a game
  57–8
    competitiveness 155
    courage on the pitch
  45, 57
    Danny Blanchflower on
  48–9
    'double-jointed ankles'
  50
    genius 45
    giftedness 43–4, 140,
  184
    goal-scoring ability
  46
    Matt Busby on 46–8
    Paddy Crerand on
  45–6, 51

party pieces/show-
boating 52–3
selfish player 54–5, 177
trouble causing on the
pitch 56–7
and the 'footballer as brand'
concept 63
friendship with Parkinson ix,
x, xiii, xvi, 83, 100–2,
128, 152–3, 171–2
funeral at Stormont Castle,
Belfast xiii, 151–2
and the gambling 89, 90–2,
99, 121–2, 168
game-changing nature of
60–4
glamour 63
and happiness 170
hatred of dancing 135
hero, Zorro 53
on his mum's alcoholism
140–2, 164, 166
on how he would like to
be remembered 149,
172
influence on football 171
and the ladies xii, xiv, 67–8,
84–6, 88–9, 92–3,
96–101, 108, 117, 123–5,
134–5, 147–8, 155, 156,
157, 159–60, 163, 166,
168, 180, 181, 187

lodges with Paddy Crerand
157–62
love of children 108, 125,
181
lowest point 143
and Manchester United xvii,
xviii, 54–5, 74, 112
1964 season 58–9
1966 season 60
arrival at the club aged
fifteen 44
brand 39
debut, 1963 ix, 57
European Cup 1968
75–7, 82
fame 67–8
first professional game,
aged seventeen 44
football zenith, 1968
xix, 83
on the good years
117–18
issued free transfer
112–14
resignations 81, 82,
102–9, 111, 169
response to the team's
post-68 decline 155–6,
164–5, 183–4
reunions xiii
shuns training 85–6,
93, 94, 96–7, 104, 112